Kawaii Amigurumi
28 Cute Animal Crochet Patterns *by Sayjai Thawornsupacharoen*

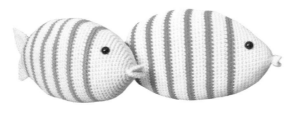

From the series : Sayjai's Amigurumi Crochet Patterns, volume 5

K and J Publishing, 16 Whitegate Close, Swavesey, Cambridge CB24 4TT, England

2

Animal Friends - page 7

Mini Gang - page 9

White Bunnies - page 18

Bride & Groom - page 21

Bobby Bear - page 11

Cat - page 32

Chubby Bear - page 27

Mouse - page 31

Leo the Lion - page 13

Cheeky Monkey - page 24

Baby Bear - page 56

Froggy - page 46

Baby Bunny - page 54

Sammy the Dog - page 43

Huggy & Funny Bunnies - page 49

Sea Animal Patterns - page 34-42

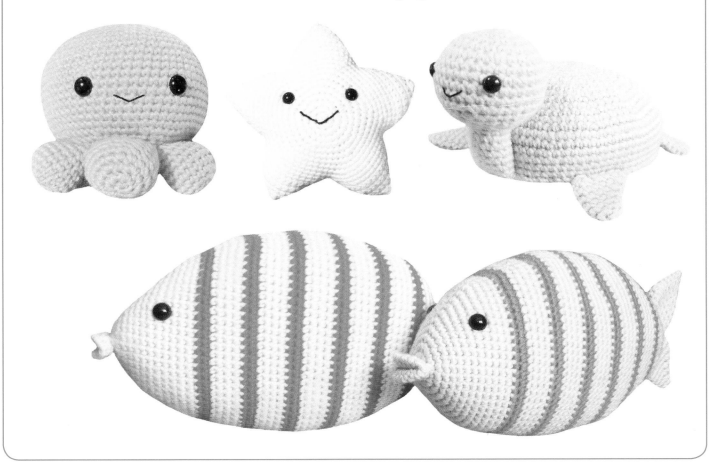

Introduction

Kawaii Amigurumi is a collection of cute amimal crochet patterns. They come in different sizes from tiny as 2 inches to a huggable 15 inch doll. The animals are: dogs, bunnies, bears, monkey, lion, cats, frogs, mouse, pig, octopus, turtle, starfish and fish.

The small dolls would be a perfect little gift for friends. The Bride & Groom dolls are a great wedding gift. Baby Bunny & Baby Bear with an easy Baby Blanket can be a baby shower gift plus many more animal dolls for boys and girls. You need a basic knowledge of crochet to read the patterns.

Size:

- The small dolls are 2 to 4.5 inches/ 5 to 7.5 cm tall.
- The medium dolls are 6 to 10.4 inches/ 15 to 26 cm tall.
- The big dolls are 10 to 15 inches/ 25 to 37.5 cm tall.

The size of the doll depends on the size of the crochet hook, the thickness of yarn and how you stuff it; a bigger hook and thicker yarn make a bigger doll. A doll stuffed tightly is bigger than a loose stuffed doll.

Abbreviations

This book uses USA crochet terminology.

ch = chain
sc = single crochet
hdc = half double crochet
dc = double crochet
st = stitch
sl = slip
rnd = round
tog = together

Conversion chart for USA/ UK crochet abbreviations:

USA Crochet Abbreviations	UK Crochet Abbreviations
sc = single crochet	dc = double crochet
hdc = half double crochet	htr = half treble crochet
dc = double crochet	tr = treble crochet

Yarn

You can use DMC Petra No 3 instead of Catania yarn from Schachenmayr SMC (see the comparison color chart for Catania & DMC Petra on page 60).

Bear & Cat
How to embroider mouth & nose.

For the first round: you can do 6 sc in magic ring instead of "Ch 2, 6 sc in second chain from hook."

Diagram of how to connect legs together.

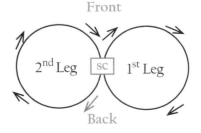

Front

2nd Leg   sc   1st Leg

Back

The sc is for connecting legs together and go through both legs. The next sc only go through second leg then go round.

Animal Friends

Materials

- Sport, Baby **fine** ② Schachenmayr Catania:
  Linen 248 = 10 g, Pool 165 = 1 g, Orchid 222 = 1 g,
  Light Pink 246 = 10 g, Raspberry 256 = 1 g,
  White 106 = 20 g, Apple Green 205 = 10 g,
  Tangerine 281 = 1 g, Turquoise 146 = 1 g and
  a little bit of Cream 130 for Bear's muzzle
- 3.00 mm hook
- Black embroidery floss
- Polyester fiberfill = 50 g
- 10 of 5 mm black beads for eyes
- Tapestry needle
- Sewing needle and thread for attaching eyes

Size

Animals are 2.5 inches/ 6.25 cm high (excluding ears).

Note

Animals have same basic patterns; Legs, Arms, Head and Body.

Animals	Skin color	Shirt color
Piglet	Light Pink 246	Raspberry 256
Bear	Linen 248	Pool 165
Bunny	White 106	Orchid 222
Frog	Apple Green 205	Tangerine 281
Puppy	White 106	Turquoise 146

Leg

Make 2 for each animal

Rnd 1: With **apple green 205** (skin color), ch 2, 6 sc in second chain from hook. (6)
Rnd 2: (Sc in next st, 2 sc in next st) around. (9)
Rnd 3-4: Sc in each st around.

For first leg, join with sl st in first st. Fasten off.
For second leg, do not sl st in first st.
Do not fasten off.

Body

Rnd 1: Hold legs together, insert hook in the last round of first leg, pull out the loop from second leg, ch 1, sc in same st (do not count this st, just for connecting legs together), sc in next 8 sts on second leg (mark first st), sc in next 8 sts on first leg, changing to **tangerine 281** (shirt color) in last 2 loops of last st. (16) See diagram of how to connect legs together on page 6.

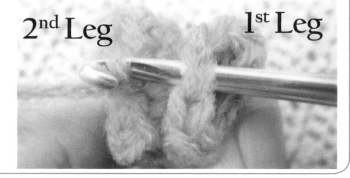

2ⁿᵈ Leg **1ˢᵗ Leg**

8

Rnd 2: Sc in next 3 sts, 2 sc in next st, sc in next 7 sts, 2 sc in next st, sc in next 4 sts. (18)
Rnd 3-4: Sc in each st around.
Rnd 5: (Sc in next st, sc next 2 sts tog) around, join with sl st in first st. Leave long end for sewing, fasten off. Stuff. (12)

Head
Make one for each animal.
Rnd 1: With **apple green 205** (skin color), ch 2, 6 sc in second chain from hook. 6)
Rnd 2: 2 sc in each st around. (12)
Rnd 3: (Sc in next st, 2 sc in next st) around. (18)
Rnd 4: (2 sc in next st, sc in next 2 sts) around. (24)
Rnd 5: (Sc in next 3 sts, 2 sc in next st) around. (30)
Rnd 6: Sc in each st around.
Rnd 7: (Sc in next 4 sts, 2 sc in next st) around. (36)
Rnd 8-9: Sc in each st around.
Rnd 10: (Sc in next 4 sts, sc next 2 sts tog) around.(30)
Rnd 11: (Sc in next 3 sts, sc next 2 sts tog) around.(24)
Rnd 12: (Sc in next 2 sts, sc next 2 sts tog) around.(18)
Rnd 13: (Sc in next st, sc next 2 sts tog) around, join with sl st in first st. Fasten off. (12)
Stuff head and sew to the body.

Arm
Make 2 for each animal, do not stuff arms.
Rnd 1: With **apple green 205** (skin color), ch 2, 6 sc in second chain from hook. (6)
Rnd 2: Sc in each st around, changing to **tangerine 281** (shirt color) in last 2 loops of last st.
Rnd 3: Sc in each st around.
Rnd 4: Sc in each st around, sl st in first st. Fasten off. Sew arms to body.

Frog
Frog Eye
Make 2.
Rnd 1: With **apple green 205**, ch 2, 6 sc in second chain from hook. (6)
Rnd 2: (Sc in next st, 2 sc in next st) around. (9)
Rnd 3: Sc in each st around, join with sl st in first st. Fasten off. Sew beads in middle of eyes.

Finishing
Sew eyes on rnds 3-5 of head. With **black** embroidery floss, embroider mouth (see page 59).

Bear

Bear Ear
Make 2.
Rnd 1: With **linen 248**, ch 2, 5 sc in second chain from hook. (5)
Rnd 2: 2 sc in each st around. (10)
Rnd 3: Sc in each st around, join with sl st in first st. Fasten off.

Bear Muzzle
Rnd 1: With **cream 130**, ch 2, 6 sc in second chain from hook. (6)
Rnd 2: (Sc in next st, 2 sc in next st) around, join with sl st in first st. Fasten off. (9)
With **black** embroidery floss, embroider nose and mouth (see page 6).

Finishing
Sew ears on rnds 4-8 of head. Sew eyes 6 sts apart between rnds 6-7 of head. Sew muzzle on rnds 6-9.

Bunny
Ear
Make 2.
Rnd 1: With **white 106**, ch 2, 6 sc in second chain from hook. (6)
Rnd 2: 2 sc in each st around. (12)
Rnd 3: (Sc in next st, 2 sc in next st) around. (18)
Rnd 4-7: Sc in each st around.
Rnd 8: (Sc next 2 sts tog, sc in next st) around. (12)
Rnd 9: Sc in each st around.
Rnd 10: Sc next 2 sts tog around. (6)
Rnd 11: Sc in each st around, join with sl st in first st, leave long end for sewing, fasten off.

Finishing
Fold ear in half and sew. Hold 2 ears together and sew. Sew ears on middle top of head. Sew eyes 6 sts apart between rnds 8-9 of head.

Piglet

Pig Snout
Rnd 1: With **light pink 246**, ch 2, 6 sc in second chain from hook. (6)
Rnd 2: Sc in each st around, join with sl st in first st. Fasten off. With **black** embroidery floss, embroider 2 lines on nose as in picture on the right.

Pig Ear
Make 2.
Rnd 1: With **light pink 246**, ch 2, 6 sc in second chain from hook. (6)
Rnd 2: Sc in each st around.
Rnd 3: (Sc in next st, 2 sc in next st) around, join with sl st in first st. Fasten off. (9)

Finishing
Sew ears on rnds 3-5 of head. Sew eyes 6 sts apart between rnds 6-7 of head. Sew snout on rnds 7-9.

Puppy

Puppy Ear
Make 2.
Rnd 1: With **black 110**, ch 2, 6 sc in second chain from hook. (6)
Rnd 2: (Sc in next st, 2 sc in next st) around. (9)
Rnd 3: Sc in each st around.
Rnd 4: (Sc next 2 sts tog, sc in next st) around. (6)
Rnd 5: Sc in each st around, join with sl st in first st. Fasten off.

Finishing
Sew ears on rnds 7 of head. Sew eyes 6 sts apart between rnds 8-9 of head.

Mini Gang

Materials

- Sport, Baby **2 fine** Schachenmayr Catania: Raspberry 256 = 5 g, Orchid 222 = 5 g, White 106 = 5 g, Apple Green 205 = 5 g, Yellow (mimosa) 100 = 5 g, Tangerine 281 = 5 g, Blue (sky) 247 = 5 g, Light blue 173 = 5 g, Chocolate 162 =5 g and a little bit of Cream 130 for Bear's muzzle.
- 3.00 mm hook
- 8 of 4 mm Black Glass Beads for eyes
- Polyester fiberfill = 20 g
- Tapestry needle
- Sewing needle and thread for attaching eyes
- Black embroidery floss

Size
Mini Gang are 2 inches/ 5 cm high (excluding ears).

Note
Mini Gang have same basic patterns; Head, Body and Scarf.

	Head color	Body color
Frog	Apple Green	Yellow (mimosa) & Tangerine
Bear	Chocolate	Light Blue & Blue (sky)
Rabbit	Orchid	Raspberry & White
Cat	Tangerine	Raspberry & Apple Green

Head & Body

Working from top of the Head to bottom of the Body.

Rnd 1: With **orchid 222**, ch 2, 6 sc in second chain from hook. (6)

Rnd 2: 2 sc in each st around. (12)

Rnd 3: (Sc in next st, 2sc in next st) around. (18)

Rnd 4: (Sc in next 2 sts, 2sc in next st) around. (24)

Rnd 5-9: Sc in each st around. (24)

Rnd 10: (Sc in next 2 sts, sc next 2 sts tog) around.(18)

Rnd 11: (Sc in next st, sc next 2 sts tog) around. (12)

Rnd 12: Sc next 2 sts tog around, changing to **raspberry 256** in last 3 loops of last st. (6)

Rnd 13: **Body:** 2sc in each st around, changing to **white 106** in last 2 loops of last st. (12)

Rnd 14: Sc in each st around changing to **raspberry 256** in last 2 loops of last st. Stuff. (12)

Rnd 15: Sc in each st around changing to **white 106** in last 2 loops of last st. (12)

Rnd 16: Sc in each st around changing to **raspberry 256** in last 2 loops of last st. Stuff. (12)

Rnd 17: Sc next 2 sts tog around, sl st in first st. Fasten off. Sew opening close. (6)

Scarf:

Make one each in raspberry, tangerine, blue (sky) and apple green. Ch 30, fasten off.

Bear

Bear Ears

Make 2.

Rnd 1: With **chocolate 162**, ch 2, 6 sc in second chain from hook. (6)

Rnd 2: (2 sc in next st, sc in next st) around. (9)

Rnd 3: Sc in each st around, join with sl st in first st. Fasten off.

Muzzle

With **cream 130**, ch 2, 6 sc in second chain from hook, join with sl st in first st. Fasten off. (6)

With **black** embroidery floss, embroider nose and mouth.

Finishing

Sew ears on rnds 4-7 of head. Sew muzzle on rnds 7-9. Sew eyes 6 sts apart between rnds 6-7 of head.

Frog

Frog Eye

Make 2.

Rnd 1: With **apple green 205**, ch 2, 6 sc in second chain from hook. (6)

Rnd 2: Sc in each st around.

Rnd 3: (Sc in next st, 2 sc in next st) around, join with sl st in first st. Fasten off. (9)

Finishing

Sew beads in middle of eyes. Sew eyes on rnds 2-5 of head. With **black** embroidery floss, embroider mouth on rnd 5.

Rabbit

Rabbit Ear

Make 2.

Rnd 1: With **orchid 222**, ch 2, 6 sc in second chain from hook. (6)

Rnd 2: (2 sc in next st, sc in next st) around. (9)

Rnd 3-4: Sc in each st around. (9)

Rnd 5: (Sc next 2 sts tog, sc in next st) around. (6)

Rnd 6: Sc in each st around.

Rnd 7: Sc in each st around, join with sl st in first st. Fasten off.

Finishing

Sew ears on rnds 3-4 of head. Sew eyes 5 sts apart between rnds 5-6 of head. With **black** embroidery floss, embroider mouth on rnd 7.

Cat

Cat Ears

Make 2.

Rnd 1: With **tangarine 281**, ch 2, 4 sc in second chain from hook. (4)

Rnd 2: (Sc in next st, 2 sc in next st) 2 times. (6)

Rnd 3: (2 sc in next st, sc in next st) around, join with sl st in first st. Fasten off. (9)

Finishing

Sew ears on rnds 3-5 of head. Sew eyes 5 sts apart between rnds 6-7 of head. With **black** embroidery floss, embroider nose on rnd 7, mouth on rnd 9.

Bobby Bear

Body

Rnd 1: With **brown 011**, ch 2, 6 sc in second chain from hook. (6)
Rnd 2: 2 sc in each st around. (12)
Rnd 3: (Sc in next st, 2 sc in next st) around. (18)
Rnd 4: (2 sc in next st, sc in next 2 sts) around. (24)
Rnd 5: (Sc in next 3 sts, 2 sc in next st) around. (30)
Rnd 6: Sc in each st around.
Rnd 7: Sc in each st around, changing to **white 001** in last 2 loops of last st.
Rnd 8: Sc in each st around.
Rnd 9: Working in back loops only. Sc in each st around, changing to **red 030** in last 2 loops of last st.
Rnd 10: (Sc next 2 sts tog, sc in next 3 sts) around, changing to **white 001** in last 2 loops of last st. (24)
Rnd 11: Sc in each st around, changing to **red 030** in last 2 loops of last st.
Rnd 12: Sc in each st around, changing to **white 001** in last 2 loops of last st.
Rnd 13: Sc in each st around, changing to **red 030** in last 2 loops of last st.
Rnd 14: (Sc next 2 sts tog, sc in next 2 sts) around, changing to **white 001** in last 2 loops of last st. (18)
Rnd 15: Sc in each st around. Leave long end for sewing, fasten off. (18)

Edge of shirt

Rnd 1: Join **red 030** to free loop of rnd 8, ch 1, sc in same st, sc in each st around, changing to **white 001** in last 2 loops of last st. (30)
Rnd 2: Sc in each st around, join with sl st in first st. Fasten off. Stuff body.

Materials

- DK, Light Worsted **[3 light]**
  Cotton Time from Schachenmayr: Red 030 = 10 g, White 001 = 10 g and Brown 011 = 50 g
- 4.00 mm hook
- Polyester fiberfill = 50 g
- Tapestry needle
- Two 6mm Black Beads for eyes
- Black embroidery floss
- 2 cm Heart Button for decoration (optional)
- Sewing needle and thread for attaching eyes and button

Yarns: you can also use 2 strands of DMC Petra No3 or 2 strands of Catania and 4 mm hook.

Size

Bobby Bear is 7 inches (17.5 cm) tall.

Head

Rnd 1: With **brown 011**, ch 2, 6 sc in second chain from hook. (6)
Rnd 2: 2 sc in each st around. (12)
Rnd 3: (Sc in next st, 2 sc in next st) around. (18)
Rnd 4: (2 sc in next st, sc in next 2 sts) around. (24)
Rnd 5: (Sc in next 3 sts, 2 sc in next st) around. (30)
Rnd 6: (Sc in next 4 sts, 2 sc in next st) around. (36)
Rnd 7: (2 sc in next st, sc in next 5 sts) around. (42)
Rnd 8: (Sc in next 6 sts, 2 sc in next st) around. (48)
Rnd 9: Sc in each st around.
Rnd 10: (Sc in next 7 sts, 2 sc in next st) around. (54)
Rnd 11: Sc in each st around.
Rnd 12: (Sc in next 8 sts, 2 sc in next st) around. (60)
Rnd 13-17: Sc in each st around.
Rnd 18: (Sc in next 8 sts, sc next 2 sts tog) around. (54)
Rnd 19: Sc in each st around.
Rnd 20: Sc in next 3 sts, sc next 2 sts tog, (sc in next 7 sts, sc next 2 sts tog) 5 times, sc in next 4 sts. (48)
Rnd 21: Sc in each st around.
Rnd 22: Sc in next 6 sts, sc next 2 sts tog, (sc in next 3 sts, sc next 2 sts tog) 2 times, sc in next 12 sts, sc next 2 sts tog, (sc in next 3 sts, sc next 2 sts tog) 2 times, sc in next 6 sts. (42)
Rnd 23: Sc in next 6 sts, sc next 2 sts tog, (sc in next 2 sts, sc next 2 sts tog) 2 times, sc in next 11 sts, sc next 2 sts tog, (sc in next 2 sts, sc next 2 sts tog) 2 times, sc in next 5 sts. (36)
Rnd 24: Sc in next 5 sts, sc next 2 sts tog, (sc in next st, sc next 2 sts tog) 2 times, sc in next 10 sts, sc next 2 sts tog, (sc in next st, sc next 2 sts tog) 2 times, sc in next 5 sts. (30)
Rnd 25: Sc in next 5 sts, (sc next 2 sts tog) 3 times, sc in next 9 sts, (sc next 2 sts tog) 3 times, sc in next 4 sts. (24)
Rnd 26: (Sc in next 2 sts, sc next 2 sts tog) around, join with sl st in first st. Fasten off. (18)
Stuff head, sew head to body.

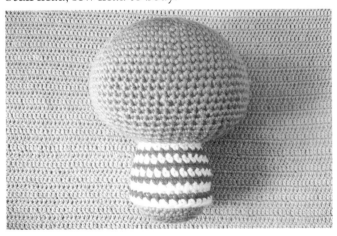

Arm

Make 2, do not stuff.

Rnd 1: With **brown 011**, ch 2, 6 sc in second chain from hook. (6)
Rnd 2-5: Sc in each st around.
Rnd 6: Sc in each st around, join with sl st in first st, fasten off.
Sew arms to body on rnd 15.

Foot and Leg

Make 2, only stuff feet.

Rnd 1: With **brown 011**, ch 4, sc in second chain from hook, sc in next ch, 3 sc in last ch; working in remaining loops on opposite side of chain, sc in next ch, 2 sc in next ch. (8)

	x	x	x	o		
x	o	o	o	x		x = sc
	x	x	x			o = chain

Rnd 2: 2 sc in next st, sc in next st, 2 sc in next 3 sts, sc in next st, 2 sc in next 2 sts. (14)
Rnd 3: <u>Working in back loops only.</u>
Sc in each st around. (14)
Rnd 4: Sc in next 3 sts, (sc next 2 sts tog) 4 times, sc in next 3 sts. (10)
Rnd 5: Sc in next st, (sc next 2 sts tog) 4 times, sc in next st. Stuff foot. (6)
Rnd 6-8: Sc in each st around.
Rnd 9: Sc in each st around, join with sl st in first st. Leave long end for sewing, fasten off.
Sew legs on rnd 5 of the body.

Ear
Make 2.
Rnd 1: With **brown 011**, ch 2, 6 sc in second chain from hook. (6)
Rnd 2: 2 sc in each st around. (12)
Rnd 3: (Sc in next 2 sts, 2 sc in next st) 4 times. (16)
Rnd 4-5: Sc in each st around.
Rnd 6: (Sc in next 2 sts, sc next 2 sts tog) around, join with sl st in first st. Leave long end for sewing, fasten off. (12)

Pin ears over rnds 7-13 of head and sew.

Muzzle
Rnd 1: With **white 001**, ch 2, 9 sc in second chain from hook, join with sl st in first st. Leave long end for sewing, fasten off. (9) With **black** embroidery floss, embroider nose and mouth (see pictures on page 6).

Finishing
Sew eyes 8 sts apart between rnds 16-17 of head.
Sew muzzle on rnds 17-20 of head.
Sew Heart Button on middle front of the body.

Leo the Lion

Materials

- Sport, Baby
  Catania yarn from Schachenmayr SMC:
  Jaffa 189 (dark orange) = 40 g, White 106 = 10 g,
  Black 110 = 10 g and Tangerine 281 = 30 g
- 3.00 mm hook
- Black embroidery floss
- Polyester fiberfill = 30 g
- Tapestry needle
- Iron wire 7 inches long
- One pair of 12 mm amber cat safety eyes

Size
Leo the Lion is 6 inches tall including the hair (15 cm).

Foot and Leg

Make 2.

Rnd 1: With **tangerine 281** (skin color), ch 2, 6 sc in second chain from hook. (6)

Rnd 2: 2 sc in each st around. (12)

Rnd 3: (Sc in next st, 2 sc in next st) around. (18)

Rnd 4: (2 sc in next st, sc in next 2 sts) around. (24)

Rnd 5: <u>Working in back loops only</u>. Sc in each st around.

Rnd 6: Sc in next 10 sts, (sc next 2 sts tog) 4 times, sc in next 6 sts.(20)

Rnd 7: (Sc next 2 sts tog, sc in next 2 sts) 2 times, (sc next 2 sts tog) 5 times, sc in next 2 sts. (13)

Rnd 8-12: Sc in each st around.

Rnd 13: Sc in each st around, changing to **black 110** (pants color) in last 2 loops of last st.

Rnd 14-15: Sc in each st around.

For first leg, join with sl st in first st. Fasten off.
For second leg, do not sl st in first st.
Do not fasten off.

Body

Rnd 1: Hold legs together with upper inner thighs together and toes pointed forward. Insert hook in the center on innermost thigh of first leg, pull out the loop from second leg, ch 1, sc in same st (do not count this st just for connecting legs together), sc in next 12 sts on second leg (mark first st), sc in next 12 sts on first leg. Stuff.(24) See diagram of how to connect legs together on page 6.

1ˢᵗ leg

2ⁿᵈ leg

Rnd 2: Sc in each st around.

Rnd 3: Sc in each st around, changing to **jaffa 189** (dark orange, shirt color) in last 2 loops of last st.

Rnd 4-10: Sc in each st around.

Rnd 11: (Sc next 2 sts tog, sc in next 2 sts) around. (18)

Rnd 12: (Sc next 2 sts tog, sc in next st) around. Leave long end for sewing, fasten off. (12) Stuff body.

Head

Rnd 1: With **tangerine 281** (skin color), ch 2, 6 sc in second ch from hook. (6)

Rnd 2: 2 sc in each st around. (12)

Rnd 3: (Sc in next st, 2 sc in next st) around. (18)

Rnd 4: (Sc in next 2 sts, 2 sc in next st) around. (24)

Rnd 5: (2 sc in next st, sc in next 3 sts) around. (30)

Rnd 6: (Sc in next 4 sts, 2 sc in next st) around. (36)

Rnd 7: (2 sc in next st, sc in next 5 sts) around. (42)

Rnd 8: (Sc in next 6 sts, 2sc in next st) around. (48)

Rnd 9: (2 sc in next st, sc in next 7 sts) around. (54)

Rnd 10-16: Sc in each st around.

Rnd 17: Sc in next 7 sts, sc next 2 sts tog, sc in next 3 sts, changing to **white 106**; with **white 106**, sc next 2 sts tog, sc in next 7 sts, sc next 2 sts tog, sc in next 11 sts, sc next 2 sts tog, changing to **tangerine 281**; with **tangerine 281**, (sc in next 7 sts, sc next 2 sts tog) 2 times. (48)

Rnd 18: Sc in next 6 sts, sc next 2 sts tog, sc in next 3 sts, changing to **white 106**; with **white 106**, sc next 2 sts tog, sc in next 9 sts, sc next 2 sts tog, sc in next 6 sts, sc next 2 sts tog, changing to **tangerine 281**; with **tangerine 281**, (sc in next 6 sts, sc next 2 sts tog) 2 times. (42)

Rnd 19: Sc in next 5 sts, sc next 2 sts tog, sc in next 3 sts, changing to **white 106**; with **white 106**, (sc next 2 sts tog, sc in next 6 sts) 2 times, sc next 2 sts tog, changing to **tangerine 281**; with **tangerine 281**, (sc in next 5 sts, sc next 2 sts tog) 2 times. (36)

Rnd 20: Sc in next 4 sts, sc next 2 sts tog, sc in next 3 sts, changing to **white 106**; with **white 106**, sc next 2 sts tog, sc in next 5 sts, sc next 2 sts tog, sc in next 4 sts, sc next 2 sts tog, changing to **tangerine 281**; with **tangerine 281**, (sc in next 4 sts, sc next 2 sts tog) 2 times. (30)

Rnd 21: Sc in next 3 sts, sc next 2 sts tog, sc in next 3 sts, changing to **white 106**; with **white 106**, sc next 2 sts tog, (sc in next 3 sts, sc next 2 sts tog) 2 times, changing to **tangerine 281**; with **tangerine 281**, (sc in next 3 sts, sc next 2 sts tog) 2 times. (24)

Rnd 22: (Sc next 2 sts tog, sc in next 2 sts) around. (18)

Stuff half of the head. Put eyes 7 sts apart between rnds 14-15.

Continue to make Rnd 23

Rnd 23: (Sc in next st, sc next 2 sts tog) around, join with sl st in first st, fasten off. (12) Stuff head tightly.

With **black** embroidery floss, embroider nose and mouth. Sew head to the body.

Arm
Make 2.

Rnd 1: With **jaffa 189** (dark orange, shirt color), ch 2, 6 sc in second chain from hook. (6)
Rnd 2: (Sc in next st, 2 sc in next st) around. (9)
Rnd 3: Sc in each st around.
Rnd 4: Sc in each st around, changing to **tangerine 281** (skin color) in last 2 loops of last st.
Rnd 5-9: Sc in each st around. Stuff.
Rnd 10: (2 sc in next st, sc in next 2 sts) around. (12)
Rnd 11: For **thumb**, sc in next 2 sts, skip next 8 sts, sc in next 2 sts, join with sl st in first st.
Fasten off. (4)

Rnd 11: For **hand**, join **tangerine 281** (skin color) to next free st on rnd 10, ch 1, sc in same st, sc in each st around. (8)
Rnd 12: Sc in each st around.
Row 13: Working in rows, flatten last rnd, matching sts and working through both thicknesses, sc in next 2 sts, sl st in next st. Fasten off.

Row 13									c	x	x	
Rnd 12			x	x	x	x	x	x	x	x		
Rnd 11	x	x	x	x	x	x	x	x	x	x	x	x
Rnd 10	x	x	x	x	x	x	x	x	x	x	x	x

Pink = hand   x = sc
Black = thumb   c = slip stitch

Sew arms to body with thumb towards front.

Ear
Make 2.

Rnd 1: With **tangerine 281** (ear color), ch 2, 6 sc in second chain from hook. (6)
Rnd 2: Sc in each st around, join with sl st in first st. Leave long end for sewing, fasten off.
Pin ears on side of head on rnds 14-15 and sew.

Hair
Make 23.

Rnd 1: With **jaffa 189** (hair color), ch 2, 4 sc in second chain from hook. (4)
Rnd 2: (2 sc in next st, sc in next st) 2 times. (6)
Rnd 3: (2 sc in next st, sc in next 2 sts) 2 times. (8)
Rnd 4: (2 sc in next st, sc in next 3 sts) 2 times. (10)
Rnd 5: (2 sc in next st, sc in next 4 sts) 2 times. (12)
Rnd 6-10: Sc in each st around.
Row 11: Working in rows, flatten last rnd, matching sts and working through both thicknesses, sc in next 5 sts, fasten off.

1) Pin 6 pieces of hair on rnd 11 of head, between ears on back of head and sew.

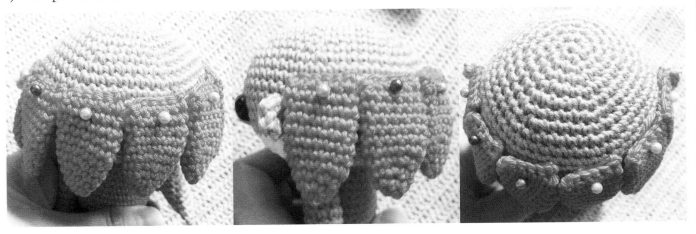

2) Pin 5 pieces of hair on rnd 8 of head, between ears on back of head and sew.

3) Pin 5 pieces of hair as in pictures below and sew.

4) Pin 2 pieces of hair as in pictures and sew.

5) Pin 2 pieces of hair as in pictures below and sew.

6) Pin 1 piece of hair as in pictures and sew.

7) Pin 1 piece of hair as in pictures and sew.

8) Pin 1 piece of hair as in pictures below and sew.

Tail
Do not stuff tail.

Rnd 1: With **tangerine 281** (tail color), ch 2,
6 sc in second chain from hook. (6)
Rnd 2-4: <u>Working in back loops only;</u>
sc in each st around. (6)
Rnd 5-19: Sc in each st around. (6)
Rnd 20: Sc in each st around, join with sl st in first st.
Leave long end for sewing, fasten off.

<u>Hair on tail</u>
Cut 18 pieces of **jaffa 189** yarn 1.5" (4 cm) long.
Hold one strand of yarn, fold in half, insert hook
through free loops of rnds 1-3 of tail, draw the folded
end through the stitch and pull the loose ends through
the folded end, draw the knot up tightly. Use needle
to split the yarns.

Finishing
Tail: Fold iron wire in half, insert it through 2 sts on rnd 2 of body at middle back, twist the wire up together and fold them at the end, put iron wire inside the tail, sew tail to body.

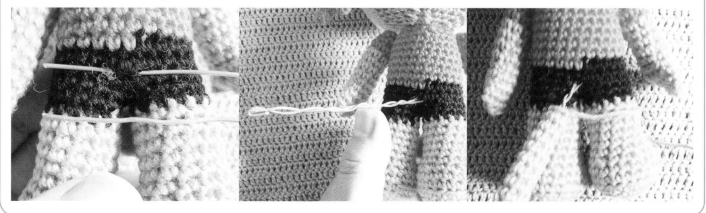

White Bunnies

Materials

For 3 bunnies.

- Sport, Baby fine
  Catania yarn from
  Schachenmayr SMC:
  White 106 = 90 g,
  Mimosa 100 (light yellow) = 10 g,
  Canary 208 (dark yellow) = 10 g,
  Raspberry 256 = 10g and
  Pool 165 (blue) = 10 g
- 3.00 mm hook
- Polyester fiberfill = 90 g
- 3 pairs of 10 mm safety eyes
- Tapestry needle

Size

Bunnies are 6 inches (15 cm) tall
(excluding ears)

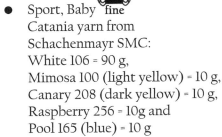

Foot and Leg

Make 2 for each bunny.

Rnd 1: With **white 106**, ch 2, 6 sc in second chain from hook. (6 sc made)
Rnd 2: 2 sc in each st around. (12)
Rnd 3: (Sc in next st, 2 sc in next st) around. (18)
Rnd 4: (2 sc in next st, sc in next 2 sts) around. (24)
Rnd 5: Sc in each st around.
Rnd 6: Sc in next 10 sts, (sc next 2 sts tog) 4 times, sc in next 6 sts. (20)
Rnd 7: (Sc next 2 sts tog, sc in next 2 sts) 2 times, (sc next 2 sts tog) 5 times, sc in next 2 sts. (13)
Rnd 8-13: Sc in each st around.

For first leg, join with sl st in first st. Fasten off.
For second leg, do not sl st in first st. Do not fasten off.

Yellow dress bunny
Rnds 1-7 are in **canary 208** (dark yellow, shoes color).

Body

Rnd 1: With **white 106**, hold legs together with upper inner thighs together and toes pointed forward. Insert hook in the center on innermost thigh of **first leg**, pull out the loop from **second leg**, sc in same st (do not count this st just for connecting legs together), sc in next 12 sts on **second leg** (mark first st), sc in next 12 sts on **first leg**. (24) See diagram of how to connect legs together on page 6.

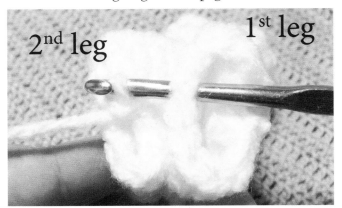

2nd leg   1st leg

Rnd 2: (Sc in next 2 sts, 2 sc in next st) around. Stuff legs. (32)
Rnd 3: Sc in each st around, changing to **pool 165** (blue, dress color) in last 2 loops of last st.
Rnd 4: (Sc in next 7 sts, 2sc in next st) around. (36)
Rnd 5: Sc in each st around.

Rnd 6: <u>Working in back loops only</u>. Sc in each st around.
Rnd 7-9: Sc in each st around.
Rnd 10: (Sc next 2 sts tog, sc in next 4 sts) around. (30)
Rnd 11: Sc in next 2 sts, sc next 2 sts tog, (sc in next 3 sts, sc next 2 sts tog) 5 times, sc in next st. (24)
Rnd 12: (Sc next 2 sts tog, sc in next 2 sts) around. (18)
Rnd 13: Sc in each st around.
Rnd 14: (Sc in next st, sc next 2 sts tog) around, join with sl st in first st, fasten off. (12)

Skirt
Rnd 1: Join **pool 165** (blue, skirt color) to free loop on rnd 5, ch 1, sc in same st, sc in each st around. (36)

Rnd 2: (Sc in next 5 sts, 2 sc in next st) around. (42)
Rnd 3: Sc in each st around.
Rnd 4: Sc in next 3 sts, 2 sc in next st, (sc in next 6 sts, 2 sc in next st) 5 times, sc in next 3 sts. (48)
Rnd 5: Sc in each st around.
Rnd 6: Sc in each st around, join with sl st in first st. Fasten off. Stuff body tightly.

Head
Rnd 1: With **white 106** (skin color). Ch 2, 6 sc in second chain from hook. (6)
Rnd 2: 2 sc in each st around. (12)
Rnd 3: (Sc in next st, 2 sc in next st) around. (18)
Rnd 4: (Sc in next 2 sts, 2 sc in next st) around. (24)
Rnd 5: (2 sc in next st, sc in next 3 sts) around. (30)
Rnd 6: Sc in next 2 sts, 2 sc in next st, (sc in next 4 sts, 2 sc in next st) 5 times, sc in next 2 sts. (36)
Rnd 7: (Sc in next 5 sts, 2 sc in next st) around. (42)
Rnd 8: Sc in next 3 sts, 2 sc in next st, (sc in next 6 sts, 2 sc in next st) 5 times, sc in next 3 sts. (48)
Rnd 9: (Sc in next 7 sts, 2 sc in next st) around. (54)
Rnd 10-16: Sc in each st around.
Rnd 17: (Sc next 2 sts tog, sc in next 7 sts) around. (48)
Rnd 18: Sc in next 3 sts, sc next 2 sts tog, (sc in next 6 sts, sc next 2 sts tog) 5 times, sc in next 3 sts. (42)
Rnd 19: (Sc in next 5 sts, sc next 2 sts tog) around. (36)

Rnd 20: Sc in next 2 sts, sc next 2 sts tog, (sc in next 4sts, sc next 2 sts tog) 5 times, sc in next 2 sts. (30)
Rnd 21: (Sc in next 3 sts, sc next 2 sts tog) around. (24)
Rnd 22: (Sc next 2 sts tog, sc in next 2 sts) around. (18)

Stuff half of the head. Put eyes 7 sts apart between rnds 14-15.
Rnd 23: (Sc in next st, sc next 2 sts tog) around, join with sl st in first st, fasten off. (12) Stuff head tightly.

Sew head to the body.

Arm
Make 2.
Rnd 1: With **white 106**, ch 2, 6 sc in second chain from hook. (6)
Rnd 2: (2 sc in next st, sc in next st) around. (9)
Rnd 3-7: Sc in each st around.
Rnd 8: Sc in each st around, changing to **pool 165** (blue, sleeve color) in last 2 loops of last st.
Rnd 9-11: Sc in each st around.
Rnd 12: Sc in each st around, join with sl st in first st. Leave long end for sewing, fasten off.
Stuff arms and sew opening close.

Sew arms to body on rnd 12 of body.

Ear
Make 2.
Rnd 1: With **white 106**, ch 2, 6 sc in second ch from hook. (6)
Rnd 2: 2 sc in each st around. (12)
Rnd 3: (Sc in next st, 2 sc in next st) around. (18)
Rnd 4: (2 sc in next st, sc in next 2 sts) around. (24)
Rnd 5-7: Sc in each st around.
Rnd 8: (Sc next 2 sts tog, sc in next 2 sts) around. (18)
Rnd 9: Sc in each st around.
Rnd 10: (Sc next 2 sts tog, sc in next st) around. (12)
Rnd 11-12: Sc in each st around.
Rnd 13: Sc in each st around, join with sl st in first st. Leave long end for sewing, fasten off. (12)

Fold ear in half and sew.

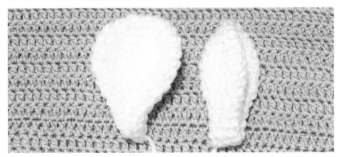

Hold 2 ears together and sew.

Sew ears on middle top of head.

Bow
Bow piece
Row 1: With **pool 165** (blue), ch 2, 3 sc in second ch from hook, turn. (3)
Row 2: Ch 1, sc in each st across, turn.
Row 3: Ch 1, 2 sc in first st, sc in next st, 2 sc in next st, turn. (5)
Row 4-8: Ch 1, sc in each st across, turn.
Row 9: Ch 1, sc first 2 sts tog, sc in next st, sc next 2 sts tog, turn. (3)
Row 10-13: Ch 1, sc in each st across, turn.
Row 14: Ch 1, 2 sc in first st, sc in next st, 2 sc in next st, turn. (5)
Row 15-19: Ch 1, sc in each st across, turn.
Row 20: Ch 1, sc first 2 sts tog, sc in next st, sc next 2 sts tog, turn. (3)
Row 21: Ch 1, sc in each st across.
Row 22: Ch 1, sc 3 sts tog, leaving long end for sewing, fasten off. (1)

Middle piece
Row 1: With **pool 165** (blue), ch 6, sc in second ch from hook, sc in next 4 chs, turn. (5)
Row 2: Ch 1, sc in each st across, leave long end for sewing, fasten off.

Sew row 1 and row 22 of bow together.
Sew the middle piece around middle of bow.

Sew bow in front of ears or on the side of head as in pictures.

Bride & Groom

Materials
For bride & groom.
- Sport, Baby Catania yarn from Schachenmayr SMC: White 106 = 50 g, Light Pink 246 = 30 g, Gray 242 = 10 g and Black 110 = 10 g
- 3.00 mm hook
- Polyester fiberfill = 60 g
- 2 pairs of 10 mm safety eyes
- Tapestry needle

Size
Bunnies are 6 inches (15 cm) tall (excluding ears)

Bride
Foot and Leg
Same as White Bunnies pattern on page 18, color white.

Body
Same as White Bunnies pattern on page 18.
Rnds 1-3: color white 106.
Rnds 4-14: color light pink 246.

Skirt
Rnd 1: Join light pink 246 to free loop on rnd 5, ch 3 (count as 1 dc), dc in next 4 sts, 2 dc in next st, (dc in next 5 sts, 2 dc in next st) 5 times, join with sl st in first st. (42)

Rnds 2-5 are working in back loops only.
Rnd 2: Ch 3 (count as 1 dc), dc in each st around, join with sl st in first st. (42)
Rnd 3: Ch 3 (count as 1 dc), dc in next 5 sts, 2 dc in next st, (dc in next 6 sts, 2 dc in next st) 5 times, join with sl st in first st. (48)

Rnd 4: Ch 3 (count as 1 dc), dc in each st around, join with sl st in first st. (48)
Rnd 5: Ch 3 (count as 1 dc), dc in next 6 sts, 2 dc in next st, (dc in next 7 sts, 2 dc in next st) 5 times, join with sl st in first st. (54)
Rnd 6: (Ch 5, sc in next st) around, fasten off.

Ruffles

Working in free loops of rnds 1-4.
Free loops of rnd 1: Join **light pink 246** to free loop on rnd 1, (Ch 5, sc in next st) around, fasten off.

Free loops of rnd 2-4: Do the same as free loops of rnd 1.

Head

Same as White Bunnies pattern on page 19, color **white**.

Arm

Same as white bunnies pattern on page 19.
Rnds 1-3: color **white 106**.
Rnds 4-12: color **light pink 246**.
Stuff arms and sew opening close. Sew arms to body on rnd 12 of body.

Ear

Same as White Bunnies pattern on page 20, color **white 106**.
Fold ear in half and sew. Hold 2 ears together and sew. Sew ears on middle top of head.
(see picture on page 20).

Bow

Same as White Bunnies pattern on page 20, color **light pink 246**.
Sew bow in front of ears.

Groom

Foot and Leg

Same as White Bunnies pattern on page 18,
Rnds 1-7: color **black 110**.
Rnds 8-13: color **gray 242**.

Body

Same as White Bunnies pattern on page 18, color **gray 242**.

Edge of shirt

Rnd 1: Join **gray 242** to free loop on rnd 5, ch 1, sc in same st, sc in each st around. (36)
Rnd 2: Sc in each st around, join with sl st in first st, fasten off. (36)

Head

Same as White Bunnies pattern on page 19, color **white 106**.

Arm

Same as White Bunnies pattern on page 19.
Rnds 1-3: color **white 106**.
Rnds 4-12: color **gray 242**.

Ear

Same as White Bunnies pattern on page 20, color white 106.
Fold ear in half and sew. Sew ears on rnd 7 of head.

Bow tie

Working in rows.

Bow

Row 1: With **Light pink 246**, ch 2, 3 sc in second chain from hook, turn. (3)
Row 2-7: Ch 1, sc in each st across, turn. (3)
Row 8: Ch 1, sc 3 sts tog, turn. (1)
Row 9: Ch 1, 3 sc in first st, turn. (3)
Row 10-15: Ch 1, sc in each st across, turn. (3)
Row 16: Ch 1, sc 3 sts tog, fasten off. (1)
Sew row 1 and row 16 together.

Middle piece

Ch 5, sc in second ch from hook, sc in next 3 chs, leave long end for sewing, fasten off. Sew the middle piece around middle of bow. Sew bow on middle front of the body (rnd 12 of body).

Hat

Rnd 1: With **black 110**, ch 2, 6 sc in second chain from hook. (6)
Rnd 2: 2 sc in each st around. (12)
Rnd 3: (2 sc in next st, sc in next st) around. (18)
Rnd 4: Working in back loops only.
Sc in each st around.
Rnd 5-9: Sc in each st around.
Rnd 10: (2 sc in next st, sc in next st) around. (27)
Rnd 11: (Sc in next 2 sts, 2 sc in next st) around, join with sl st in first st. Leave long end for sewing. Fasten off. (36)

Sew hat on top of the head, stuff hat before sewing the opening close.

Cheeky Monkey

Materials

- Sport, Baby [fine 2] Catania from Schachenmayr: Linen 248 = 15 g, Pool 165 (blue) = 10 g, Gray 242 = 1 g, Cream 130 = 5 g and a little bit of White 106 for eyes.
- Black embroidery floss
- 2 mm Black beads for eyes.
- 3.00 mm hook
- Polyester fiberfill = 20 g
- Tapestry needle
- Pins

Size

Monkey is 5.25 inches (13 cm) tall.

Body and Head

Working from bottom of body to top of head.

Rnd 1: With **linen 248** (body color), ch 2, 6 sc in second chain from hook. (6)

Rnd 2: 2 sc in next st around. (12)

Rnd 3: (Sc in next st, 2 sc in next st) around. (18)

Rnd 4: (Sc in next 2 sts, 2 sc in next st) around. (24)

Rnd 5: Sc in each st around.

Rnd 6: Sc in each st around, changing to **pool 165** (shirt color) in last 2 loops of last st.

Rnd 7-9: Sc in each st around.

Rnd 10: (Sc in next 2 sts, sc next 2 sts tog) around. (18)

Rnd 11: Sc in each st around.

Rnd 12: (Sc in next st, sc next 2 sts tog) around. (12)

Rnd 13: Sc in each st around, changing to **linen 248** (skin color) in last 2 loops of last st.

Rnd 14: 2 sc in each st around. (24)

Rnd 15: (Sc in next st, 2 sc in next st) around. (36)

Rnd 16: (Sc in next 2 sts, 2 sc in next st) around. (48)

Rnd 17-19: Sc in each st around.

Rnd 20: (Sc in next 6 sts, sc next 2 sts tog) around. (42)

Rnd 21: (Sc in next 5 sts, sc next 2 sts tog) around. (36)

Rnd 22: (Sc in next 10 sts, sc next 2 sts tog) around. (33)

Rnd 23: (Sc in next 9 sts, sc next 2 sts tog) around. (30)

Rnd 24-25: Sc in each st around.

Rnd 26: (Sc in next 3 sts, sc next 2 sts tog) around. (24)

Rnd 27: (Sc in next 2 sts, sc next 2 sts tog) around. Stuff. (18)

Rnd 28: (Sc in next st, sc next 2 sts tog) around. (12)

Rnd 29: Sc next 2 sts tog around, join with sl st in first st.

Row 30: <u>Working in rows.</u> **For hair on top**; ch 4, sc in second chain from hook, sc in next 2 chs, sc in next st, ch 6, sc in second chain from hook, sc in next 4 chs, sc in next st, ch 3, sc in second chain from hook, sc in next ch, sc in next st, sl st in next st. Fasten off. Sew the opening close.

```
                o
              xo
              xo   o
        o    xo  xo
       xo  xo  xo
       xo  xo    xo  <= Rnd 30 starts here
     c x    x    x
  x x x x      x    x   <= Rnd 29
```

x = sc   o = chain   c = sl st

Foot and Leg
Make 2, only stuff feet.

Rnd 1: With **gray 242** (shoes color), ch 4, sc in second chain from hook, sc in next ch, 3 sc in last ch; working in remaining loops on opposite side of chain, sc in next ch, 2 sc in next ch. (8)

	x	x	x	o	
x	o	o	o	x	
	x	x	x		

x = sc   o = chain

Rnd 2: 2 sc in next st, sc in next st, 2 sc in next 3 sts, sc in next st, 2 sc in next 2 sts. (14)
Rnd 3: Sc in each st around. (14)
Rnd 4: Sc in next 3 sts, (sc next 2 sts tog) 4 times, sc in next 3 sts. (10)
Rnd 5: Sc in next 2 sts, (sc next 2 sts tog) 3 times, sc in next 2 sts. (7)
Rnd 6: Sc in each st around, changing to **linen 248** (leg color) in last 2 loops of last st.
Rnd 7: Sc in each st around. Stuff foot.
Rnd 8-14: Sc in each st around.
Rnd 15: Sc in each st around, join with sl st in first st. Leave long end for sewing, fasten off.
Do not stuff legs, sew to body on rnd 5.

Arm
Make 2, do not stuff arms.

Rnd 1: With **linen 248** (arm color), ch 2, 6 sc in second chain from hook. (6)
Rnd 2-11: Sc in next st around.
Rnd 12: Sc in each st around, changing to **cream 130** (hand color) in last 2 loops of last st.
Rnd 13: Sc in each st around.
Rnd 14: For **thumb**, 2 sc in first st, skip next 4 sts, 2 sc in next st, join with sl st in first st. Fasten off.

Rnd 14: For **hand**, join **cream 130** (hand color) to next free st on rnd 13, ch 1, 2 sc in same st, 2 sc in next 3 sts. (8)
Rnd 15: Sc in each st around.
Row 16: Working in row, flatten last rnd, matching sts and working through both thicknesses, sc in next 2 sts, sl st in next st. Fasten off.

Row 16					c x x	
Rnd 15		x x	x x	x x	x x	
Rnd 14	v	v	v	v	v	v
Rnd 13	x	x	x	x	x	x

Pink = hand   x = sc   o = chain
Black = thumb   c = slip stitch

Sew arms to body with thumb towards front.

Tail
With **linen 248** (tail color), ch 23, dc in 4th chain from hook, dc in next 19 chains, leave long end for sewing, fasten off. (21)
Sew the top part and bottom part together.

Sew tail to body on rnd 5.

Eye
Make 2.

With **white 106**, ch 2, 6 sc in second chain from hook, sl st in first st. Leave long end for sewing, fasten off. (6) Sew **black** beads to middle of eyes.

Skin under eyes, make 2.

Rnd 1: With **cream 130** (skin color), ch 2, 6 sc in second chain from hook. (6)
Rnd 2: 2 sc in each st around, sl st in first st, fasten off. (12)
Sew 2 pieces of skin under eyes together.

Sew eyes on them as shown in picture.

Pin them over rnds 20-24 of head and sew.

Mouth
Rnd 1: With **cream 130** (mouth color), ch 12, sc in second chain from hook, sc in next 9 chs, 3 sc in next ch; working in remaining loops on opposite side of chain, sc in next 9 chs, 2 sc in next ch. (24)

```
    x x x x x x x x x x x o
  x o o o o o o o o o o o x
    x x x x x x x x x x x
```

o = chain   x = sc

Rnd 2: 2 sc in next st, sc in next 9 sts, 2 sc in next 3 sts, sc in next 9 sts, 2 sc in next 2 sts. (30)
Rnd 3-4: Sc in each st around.
Rnd 5: Sc in each st around, join with sl st in first st. Leave long end for sewing, fasten off.
Pins mouth over rnds 15-19 as in picture, sew it to head and stuff before sewing the opening close.

Ear
Make 2 in cream 130 and 2 in linen 248.
Rnd 1: Ch 2, 6 sc in second chain from hook, sl st in first st, fasten off. (6)

Matching sts, hold one **cream 130** ear and one **linen 248** ear together. Working in rnd 1 through both thicknesses, with **cream 130** side facing you, join **linen 248** to rnd 1 of ear, ch 1, sc in same st, 2 sc in next st, (sc in next st, 2 sc in next st) 2 times, join with sl st in first st. Leave long end for sewing, fasten off. (9)

Pin ears on rnd 21 and sew.

Finishing
With **black**, embroider mouth.

Chubby Bear

- 4 plastic washers for 9 mm safety eyes (for the barbell set)
- PVA glue
- One cleaned empty Tuna can (diameter 8.5 cm, 4.5 cm high)
- Polystyrene foam (I used packing foam.) to put in Tuna can
- Needle and thread
- Letter buttons or other decorations of your choice

Size
Bear is 5 inches (12.5 cm) tall (excluding base).

Leg
Make two.
Rnd 1: With **linen** 248, ch 2, 6 sc in second chain from hook. (6)
Rnd 2: (2 sc in next st, sc in next st) around. (9)
Rnd 3: (2 sc in next st, sc in next 2 sts) around. (12)
Rnd 4: (2 sc in next st, sc in next 3 sts) around. (15)
Rnd 5: (2 sc in next st, sc in next 4 sts) around. (18)

For first leg, join with sl st in first st. Fasten off.
For second leg, do not sl st in first st.
Do not fasten off.

Body
Rnd 1: Hold legs together. Insert hook in the center of first leg, pull out the loop from second leg, ch 1, sc in same st (do not count this st just for connecting legs together), sc in next 17 sts on second leg (mark first st), sc in next 17 sts on first leg. (34) See diagram of how to connect legs together on page 6.

Rnd 2: (2 sc in next st, sc in next 16 sts) 2 times. (36)
Rnd 3: (Sc in next 5 sts, 2 sc in next st) around. (42)

Materials

- Sport, Baby [2 fine] Schachenmayr Catania: Turquoise 146 = 25 g, Red 115 = 10 g, Black 110 = 10 g, Linen 248 = 25 g, a little bit of Silver 172 for covering the Bamboo stick and a little bit of Cream 130 for making muzzle/mouth.
  Or use DMC Petra No 3, see comparison color chart of Schachenmayr Catania and DMC Petra No3 on page 60.
- 3.00 mm hook (US: D/3 (3.25mm), UK: 11)
- Tapestry needle
- One pair of 9 mm safety eyes
- Black embroidery floss
- Polyester fibrefill = 80 g.
- Optional: One pair of Doll Glasses 2.4–2.75 inches (6–6.99 cm) wide
- Iron wire 15 cm long and 10 cm long. (One for weight bar and another one for keeping the Bear stand on the Base.)

Rnd 4: Sc in next 3 sts, 2 sc in next st, (sc in next 6 sts, 2 sc in next st) 5 times, sc in next 3 sts. (48)
Rnd 5-8: Sc in each st around.
Rnd 9: Sc in each st around, changing to **red 115** (shirt color) in last 2 loops of last st.
Rnd 10-15: Sc in each st around.
Rnd 16: Sc in next 3 sts, sc next 2 sts tog, (sc in next 6 sts, sc next 2 sts tog) 5 times, sc in next 3 sts. (42)
Rnd 17: Sc in each st around.
Rnd 18: (Sc in next 5 sts, sc next 2 sts tog) around. (36)
Rnd 19: Sc in each st around.
Rnd 20: Sc in next 2 sts, sc next 2 sts tog, (sc in next 4 sts, sc next 2 sts tog) 5 times, sc in next 2 sts. (30)
Rnd 21-22: Sc in each st around.
Rnd 23: (Sc next 2 sts tog, sc in next 3 sts) around. (24)
Rnd 24: (Sc next 2 sts tog, sc in next 2 sts) around, join with sl st in first st. Leave long end for sewing, fasten off. (18)
Stuff body tightly by using tip of scissors push the stuffing in.

Head

Rnd 1: With **linen** 248 (skin color), ch 2, 6 sc in second chain from hook. (6)
Rnd 2: 2 sc in each st around. (12)
Rnd 3: (Sc in next st, 2 sc in next st) around. (18)
Rnd 4: (Sc in next 2 sts, 2 sc in next st) around. (24)
Rnd 5: (2 sc in next st, sc in next 3 sts) around. (30)
Rnd 6: Sc in next 2 sts, 2 sc in next st, (sc in next 4 sts, 2 sc in next st) 5 times, sc in next 2 sts. (36)
Rnd 7: (Sc in next 5 sts, 2 sc in next st) around. (42)
Rnd 8: Sc in next 3 sts, 2 sc in next st, (sc in next 6 sts, 2 sc in next st) 5 times, sc in next 3 sts. (48)
Rnd 9: (Sc in next 7 sts, 2 sc in next st) around. (54)
Rnd 10-16: Sc in each st around.
Rnd 17: (Sc in next 7 sts, sc next 2 sts tog) around. (48)
Rnd 18: Sc in next 3 sts, sc next 2 sts tog, (sc in next 6 sts, sc next 2 sts tog) 5 times, sc in next 3 sts. (42)
Rnd 19: (Sc in next 5 sts, sc next 2 sts tog) around. (36)
Rnd 20: Sc in next 2 sts, sc next 2 sts tog, (sc in next 4 sts, sc next 2 sts tog) 5 times, sc in next 2 sts. (30)
Rnd 21: (Sc in next 3 sts, sc next 2 sts tog) around. (24)
Rnd 22: (Sc next 2 sts tog, sc in next 2 sts) around, join with sl st in first st, fasten off. (18)

Insert safety eyes 7-8 sts apart between rnds 14-15, stuff head tightly by using tip of scissors push the stuffing in. Sew head to body.

Arm

Make two, do not stuff arms.
Rnd 1: With **linen** 248 (skin color), ch 2, 6 sc in second chain from hook. (6)
Rnd 2-5: Sc in each st around.
Rnd 6: Sc in each st around, changing to **red 115** (sleeve color) in last 2 loops of last st.
Rnd 7-9: Sc in each st around.
Rnd 10: Sc in each st around, join with sl st in first st, leave long end for sewing, fasten off.
Sew arm on rnd 23 of the body.

Ear

Make two.
Rnd 1: With **linen** 248 (skin color), ch 2, 6 sc in second chain from hook. (6)
Rnd 2: 2 sc in each st around. (12)
Rnd 3: (2 sc in next st, sc in next 3 sts) around. (15)
Rnd 4: Sc in each st around.
Rnd 5: Sc in each st around, join with sl st in first st, leave long end for sewing, fasten off. (15)
Sew ears on rnds 10-16.

Muzzle/ Mouth

Rnd 1: With **cream 130**, ch 2, 6 sc in second chain from hook. (6)
Rnd 2: (Sc in next st, 2 sc in next st) around, leave long end for sewing, fasten off. (9)

With **black** embroidery floss, embroider nose and mouth as in pictures. Sew muzzle on rnds 15-18.

Base

Top

Rnd 1: With **turquoise 146**, ch 2,
6 sc in second ch from hook. (6)
Rnd 2: 2 sc in each st around. (12)
Rnd 3: (Sc in next st, 2 sc in next st) around. (18)
Rnd 4: (Sc in next 2 sts, 2 sc in next st) around. (24)
Rnd 5: (2 sc in next st, sc in next 3 sts) around. (30)
Rnd 6: Sc in next 2 sts, 2 sc in next st, (sc in next 4 sts, 2 sc in next st) 5 times, sc in next 2 sts. (36)
Rnd 7: (Sc in next 5 sts, 2 sc in next st) around. (42)
Rnd 8: Sc in next 3 sts, 2 sc in next st, (sc in next 6 sts, 2 sc in next st) 5 times, sc in next 3 sts. (48)
Rnd 9: (Sc in next 7 sts, 2 sc in next st) around. (54)
Rnd 10: Sc in next 4 sts, 2 sc in next st, (sc in next 8 sts, 2 sc in next st) 5 times, sc in next 4 sts. (60)
Rnd 11: (Sc in next 9 sts, 2 sc in next st) around. (66)
Rnd 12-23: Sc in each st around. (66)
Rnd 24: Sc in each st around, join with sl st in first st, fasten off. (66)

Bottom

Rnd 1: With **turquoise 146**, ch 2,
6 sc in second ch from hook. (6)
Rnd 2: 2 sc in each st around. (12)
Rnd 3: (Sc in next st, 2 sc in next st) around. (18)
Rnd 4: (Sc in next 2 sts, 2 sc in next st) around. (24)
Rnd 5: (2 sc in next st, sc in next 3 sts) around. (30)
Rnd 6: Sc in next 2 sts, 2 sc in next st, (sc in next 4 sts, 2 sc in next st) 5 times, sc in next 2 sts. (36)
Rnd 7: (Sc in next 5 sts, 2 sc in next st) around. (42)
Rnd 8: Sc in next 3 sts, 2 sc in next st, (sc in next 6 sts, 2 sc in next st) 5 times, sc in next 3 sts. (48)
Rnd 9: (Sc in next 7 sts, 2 sc in next st) around. (54)
Rnd 10: Sc in next 4 sts, 2 sc in next st, (sc in next 8 sts, 2 sc in next st) 5 times, sc in next 4 sts. (60)
Rnd 11: (Sc in next 9 sts, 2 sc in next st) around, join with sl st in first st, leave long end for sewing, fasten off. (66)

Sew the letter buttons/ decorations on the top part. Put Polystyrene foam in Tuna can, cover the can with the top part, sew the bottom part to the top part.

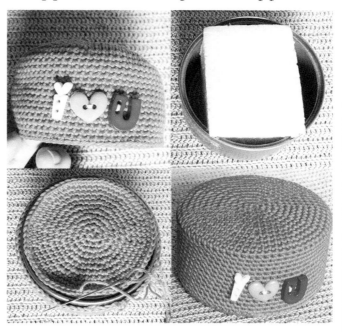

Stick the iron wire (10 cm long) in to the Bear's leg, leave iron wire sticking out about 4.5 cm, position the Bear in the middle. Put the iron wire into the Base. When you are satisfied with the Bear's position, sew Bear's legs to the Base with sewing needle and thread (same color as Bear's legs).

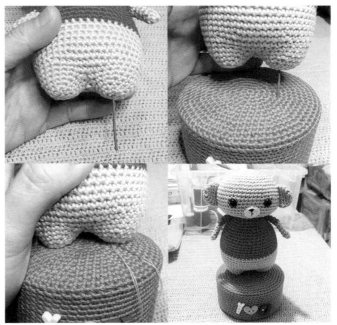

Barbell set

Weights

Make four.

Rnd 1: With **black 110**, ch 5, sl st in first ch to from a ring, ch 1, 12 sc in ring. (12)

Rnd 2: (Sc in next st, 2 sc in next st) around. (18)

Rnd 3: (Sc in next 2 sts, 2 sc in next st) around. (24)

For first and second discs, join with sl st in first st. Fasten off.

For third and fourth discs, do not sl st in first st. Do not fasten off.

Matching sts, hold **first** and **third** discs together, sc around, sl st in first st, fasten off. (24)

Matching sts, hold **second** and **fourth** discs together, sc around, sl st in first st, fasten off. (24)

Bar

Wrap the yarn (**silver 172**) around 15 cm iron wire, use glue at the beginning and the end.

Skip 2 cm from the end, wrap yarn 1 cm long, 2 layers to make that part thick so the weight would stay in place, do the same on the other side of bar.

Assembly barbell

Glue plastic washers to both weight discs as in picture, put glue on the bar, put weight on bar.

Sew Barbell set to the Bear's hands.

Glasses, cut both tips off.

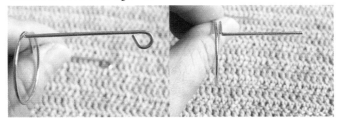

Put the glasses on Bear by using glue on both legs.

Cat & Mouse

Material

- Worsted, Afghan, Aran
  Rico Design Creative Cotton Aran yarns:
  Black 090 = 50 g, Light Green 040 = 10 g,
  Sky Blue 037 = 5 g, White 080 = 10 g,
  Light Yellow 063 = 5 g and Orange 074 = 5 g
- 4.5 mm hook (US 7, UK 7)
- DMC Pearl Cotton Thread Size 3 (115/3):
  Orange 740 = 1 skein
- DMC Pearl Cotton Thread Size 5 (115/5):
  Black 310 = 1 skein (to embroider nose and mouth)
- 3.25 mm hook (US 3/D, UK 10)
- Polyester fibrefill 75 g
- Two 4 mm black beads for mouse's eyes
- Needle for embroidery and attaching Mouse's eyes
- Tapestry needle.
- Pins

Size

- Cat is 7.5 inches/ 18.5 cm high
  (excluding ears) standing.
- Mouse is 2.5 inches/ 6.5 cm
  long
  (excluding tail).

Mouse

Body

Rnd 1: With color **white 080**, ch 2, 4 sc in second chain from hook. (4)
Rnd 2: (Sc in next st, 2 sc in next st) 2 times. (6)
Rnd 3: (Sc in next st, 2 sc in next st) around. (9)
Rnd 4: (Sc in next 2 sts, 2 sc in next st) around. (12)
Rnd 5: Sc in each st around, changing to **green 040** in last 2 loops of last st.
Rnd 6: (Sc in next st, 2 sc in next st) around, changing to **yellow 063** in last 2 loops of last st. (18)
Rnd 7: Sc in each st around, changing to **orange 074** in last 2 loops of last st.
Rnd 8: (Sc in next 2 sts, 2 sc in next st) around, changing to **green 040** in last 2 loops of last st. (24)
Rnd 9: Sc in each st around, changing to **yellow 063** in last 2 loops of last st.
Rnd 10: Sc in each st around, changing to **orange 074** in last 2 loops of last st.
Rnd 11: (Sc next 2 sts tog, sc in next 2 sts) around, changing to **green 040** in last 2 loops of last st. (18)

Rnd 12: Sc in each st around, changing to **yellow 063** in last 2 loops of last st.
Rnd 13: (Sc next 2 sts tog, sc in next st) around, changing to **orange 074** in last 2 loops of last st. Stuff. (12)
Rnd 14: Sc next 2 sts tog around, join with sl st in first st, fasten off. (6) Sew the opening close.

Tail

With DMC Pearl Cotton Thread Size 3 (115/3): **orange 740** and 3.25 mm hook, ch 20, sc in second chain from hook, sc in next 18 chs, leave long end for sewing, fasten off. (19)
Sew the top part and bottom part together.

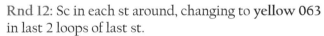

Ear
Make 2, with DMC Pearl Cotton Thread Size 3 (115/3):
orange 740 and 3.25 mm hook.
Rnd 1: Ch 2, 6 sc in second chain from hook. (6)
Rnd 2: 2 sc in each st around, join with sl st in first st,
leave long end for sewing, fasten off. (12)

Finishing
With DMC Pearl Cotton Thread Size 3 (115/3):
orange 740 embroider nose as in pictures.

Fold ear in half and sew at the bottom, see picture.

Sew ears 3 sts apart on rnd 6. Sew tail to middle of rnd
14 of body. Sew eyes 2 sts apart between rnds 3-4.

Cat
Head
Rnd 1: With **black 090**, ch 2, 6 sc in second chain from hook. (6)
Rnd 2: 2 sc in each st around. (12)
Rnd 3: (Sc in next st, 2 sc in next st) around. (18)
Rnd 4: (2 sc in next st, sc in next 2 sts) around. (24)
Rnd 5: (Sc in next 3 sts, 2 sc in next st) around. (30)
Rnd 6: (Sc in next 4 sts,2 sc in next st) around.(36)
Rnd 7: (2 sc in next st, sc in next 5 sts) around. (42)
Rnd 8: (Sc in next 6 sts, 2 sc in next st) around. (48)
Rnd 9: Sc in each st around.
Rnd 10: (Sc in next 7 sts, 2 sc in next st) around. (54)
Rnd 11: Sc in each st around.
Rnd 12: (Sc in next 8 sts, 2 sc in next st) around. (60)
Rnd 13-17: Sc in each st around.
Rnd 18: (Sc in next 8 sts, sc next 2sts tog) around. (54)
Rnd 19: Sc in each st around.
Rnd 20: (Sc in next 7 sts, sc next 2 sts tog) around. (48)
Rnd 21: Sc in each st around.
Rnd 22: (Sc in next 6 sts, sc next 2 sts tog) around. (42)
Rnd 23: (Sc in next 5 sts, sc next 2 sts tog) around. (36)
Rnd 24: (Sc in next 4 sts, sc next 2 sts tog) around. (30)
Rnd 25: (Sc in next 3 sts, sc next 2 sts tog) around. (24)
Rnd 26: (Sc in next 2 sts, sc next 2 sts tog) around,
join with sl st in first st. Fasten off. (18)
Put safety eyes 6 sts apart, between rnd 16-17 of head. Stuff.

Muzzle
Rnd 1: With **white 080**, ch 2, 9 sc in second chain from hook, join with sl st in first st. Leave long end for sewing, fasten off. (9)

With **black** embroidery floss (DMC Pearl Cotton Thread Size 5 (115/5): **black 310**), embroider nose and mouth (see pictures on page 6).
Sew muzzle on rnds 17-19 of head.

Body
Rnd 1: With **black 090**, ch 2, 6 sc in second chain from hook. (6)
Rnd 2: 2 sc in each st around. (12)
Rnd 3: (Sc in next st, 2 sc in next st) around. (18)
Rnd 4: (2 sc in next st, sc in next 2 sts) around. (24)
Rnd 5: (Sc in next 3 sts, 2 sc in next st) around. (30)
Rnd 6: Sc in each st around.
Rnd 7: Sc in each st around, changing to **blue 037** in last 2 loops of last st.
Rnd 8: Sc in each st around.
Rnd 9: <u>Working in back loops only</u>. Sc in each st around, changing to **green 040** in last 2 loops of last st.
Rnd 10: (Sc next 2 sts tog, sc in next 3 sts) around, changing to **white 080** in last 2 loops of last st. (24)
Rnd 11: Sc in each st around, changing to **blue 037** in last 2 loops of last st.
Rnd 12: Sc in each st around, changing to **green 040** in last 2 loops of last st.
Rnd 13: Sc in each st around, changing to **white 080** in last 2 loops of last st.
Rnd 14: (Sc next 2 sts tog, sc in next 2 sts) around, changing to **blue 037** in last 2 loops of last st. (18)
Rnd 15: Sc in each st around. Leave long end for sewing, fasten off. (18)

Edge of shirt
Rnd 1: Join **white 080** to free loop of rnd 8, ch 1, sc in same st, sc in each st around, changing to **green 040** in last 2 loops of last st. (30)
Rnd 2: Sc in each st around, join with sl st in first st. Fasten off.

Stuff body. Sew body to head.

Arm
Make 2 in **black 090** color, do not stuff arms.
Rnd 1: Ch 2, 6 sc in second chain from hook. (6)
Rnd 2-5: Sc in each st around.
Rnd 6: Sc in each st around, join with sl st in first st, fasten off.
Sew arms to body on rnd 14.

Leg
Make 2 in **black 090** color, only stuff feet.
Rnd 1: Ch 4, sc in second ch from hook, sc in next ch, 3 sc in last ch; working in remaining loops on opposite side of chain, sc in next ch, 2 sc in next ch. (8)

```
   x   x   x   o              o = ch
  x   o   o   o   x           x = sc
     x   x   x
```

Rnd 2: 2 sc in next st, sc in next st, 2 sc in next 3 sts, sc in next st, 2 sc in next 2 sts. (14)
Rnd 3: <u>Working in back loops only.</u>
Sc in each st around.
Rnd 4: Sc in next 3 sts, (sc next 2 sts tog) 4 times, sc in next 3 sts. (10)
Rnd 5: Sc in next st, (sc next 2 sts tog) 4 times, sc in next st. Stuff foot. (6)
Rnd 6-8: Sc in each st around.
Rnd 9: Sc in each st around, join with sl st in first st. Leave long end for sewing, fasten off.
Sew legs on rnd 5 of the body.

Tail
With **black 090**, ch 15, sc in second chain from hook, sc in next 13 chs, leave long end for sewing, fasten off. (14)
Sew the top part and bottom part together.

Sew tail to Rnd 5 of body.

Ear

Outer Ear
Make 2 in black 090 color.
Rnd 1: Ch 2, 4 sc in second chain from hook. (4)
Rnd 2: (Sc in next st, 2 sc in next st) 2 times. (6)
Rnd 3: (Sc in next st, 2 sc in next st) around. (9)
Rnd 4: (Sc in next 2 sts, 2 sc in next st) around. (12)
Rnd 5: (Sc in next 3 sts, 2 sc in next st) around. (15)
Rnd 6: Sc in each st around.
Rnd 7: Sc in each st around, join with sl st in first st.
Leave long end for sewing, fasten off. Sew the opening close flat.

Inner Ear
Make 2 in green 040 color.
Row 1: Ch 5, sc in second ch from hook,
sc in next 3 chs, turn. (4)
Row 2: Ch 1, sc in each st across, turn. (4)
Row 3: Ch 1, sc first 2 sts tog, sc next 2 sts tog, turn. (2)
Row 4: Ch 1, sc first 2 sts tog, leave long end for sewing, fasten off. (1)

Finishing
Sew inner ear on top of outer ear.

Pin and sew ears over rnds 7-12 of head.

Starfish

Materials
- DK, Light Worsted
  Robin DK: Lemon 048 = 80 g
- 5.00 mm hook
- Polyester fiberfill = 120 g
- One pair of 15 mm safety eyes
- DMC Pearl Cotton Thread
  Size 3 (115/3): Color Black 310
- Tapestry needle

Size
Starfish is 10 inches (25 cm) wide.

Note
Crochet using 2 strands of yarn and 5 mm hook.

Body
Make 2.

Rnd 1: With **lemon 048**, ch 2, 5 sc in second chain from hook. (5)
Rnd 2: 2 sc in each st around. (10)
Rnd 3: (3 sc in next st, sc in next st) around. (20)
Rnd 4: (2 sc in next st, sc in next 3 sts) around. (25)
Rnd 5: (3 sc in next st, sc in next 4 sts) around. (35)
Rnd 6: (2 sc in next st, sc in next 6 sts) around. (40)
Rnd 7: (3 sc in next st, sc in next 7 sts) around. (50)
Rnd 8: (2 sc in next st, sc in next 9 sts) around. (55)
Rnd 9: (2 sc in next st, sc in next 10 sts) around. (60)
Rnd 10: (3 sc in next st, sc in next 11 sts) around. (70)
Rnd 11: (2 sc in next st, sc in next 13 sts) around. (75)
Rnd 12: (2 sc in next st, sc in next 14 sts) around. (80)

Working in rows.
First point
Row 13: Sc in next 16 sts, turn. (16)
Row 14: Ch 1, sc first 2 sts tog, sc in next 12 sts, sc next 2 sts tog, turn. (14)
Row 15: Ch 1, sc first 2 sts tog, sc in next 10 sts, sc next 2 sts tog, turn. (12)
Row 16: Ch 1, sc first 2 sts tog, sc in next 8 sts, sc next 2 sts tog, turn. (10)
Row 17: Ch 1, sc first 2 sts tog, sc in next 6 sts, sc next 2 sts tog, turn. (8)
Row 18: Ch 1, sc first 2 sts tog, sc in next 4 sts, sc next 2 sts tog, turn. (6)
Row 19: Ch 1, sc first 2 sts tog, sc in next 2 sts, sc next 2 sts tog, turn. (4)
Row 20: Ch 1, sc first 2 sts tog, sc next 2 sts tog, turn. (2)
Row 21: Ch 1, sc first 2 sts tog, fasten off. (1)

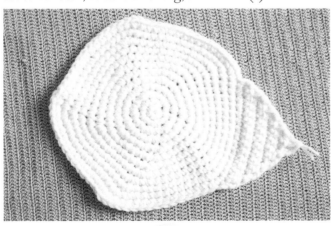

Second - Fifth points
Row 13: Join **lemon 048** to next free st on rnd 12, ch 1, sc in same st, sc in 15 sts, turn. (16)

Row 14: Ch 1, sc first 2 sts tog, sc in next 12 sts, sc next 2 sts tog, turn. (14)
Row 15: Ch 1, sc first 2 sts tog, sc in next 10 sts, sc next 2 sts tog, turn. (12)
Row 16: Ch 1, sc first 2 sts tog, sc in next 8 sts, sc next 2 sts tog, turn. (10)
Row 17: Ch 1, sc first 2 sts tog, sc in next 6 sts, sc next 2 sts tog, turn. (8)
Row 18: Ch 1, sc first 2 sts tog, sc in next 4 sts, sc next 2 sts tog, turn. (6)
Row 19: Ch 1, sc first 2 sts tog, sc in next 2 sts, sc next 2 sts tog, turn. (4)
Row 20: Ch 1, sc first 2 sts tog, sc next 2 sts tog, turn. (2)
Row 21: Ch 1, sc first 2 sts tog, fasten off. (1)

Insert eyes between rnds 6-7. Use pins to mark the mouth line. With **black** embroidery floss embroider mouth as in picture.

Hold wrong side of star together, matching points and sew 2 pieces together. Stuff before sew the opening close.

Octopus

Materials

- DK, Light Worsted
  Robin DK: Fondant 052 = 75 g
- 5.00 mm hook
- Polyester fiberfill = 125 g
- One pair of 15 mm safety eyes
- DMC Pearl Cotton Thread Size 3
  (115/3): Color Black 310
- Tapestry needle

Size

Octopus is 5 inches (12.5 cm) high.

Note

Crochet using 2 strands of yarn and
5 mm hook.

Body

Rnd 1: With **fondant 052**, ch 2, 6 sc in second chain
from hook. (6)
Rnd 2: 2 sc in each st around. (12)
Rnd 3: (Sc in next st, 2 sc in next st) around. (18)
Rnd 4: (Sc in next 2 sts, 2 sc in next st) around. (24)
Rnd 5: (2 sc in next st, sc in next 3 sts) around. (30)
Rnd 6: Sc in next 2 sts, 2 sc in next st, (sc in next 4 sts,
2 sc in next st) 5 times, sc in next 2 sts. (36)
Rnd 7: (Sc in next 5 sts, 2 sc in next st) around. (42)
Rnd 8: Sc in next 3 sts, 2 sc in next st, (sc in next 6 sts,
2 sc in next st) 5 times, sc in next 3 sts. (48)
Rnd 9: (Sc in next 7 sts, 2 sc in next st) around. (54)
Rnd 10: Sc in next 4 sts, 2 sc in next st, (sc in next 8 sts,
2 sc in next st) 5 times, sc in next 4 sts. (60)
Rnd 11: Sc in each st around.
Rnd 12: (Sc in next 9 sts, 2 sc in next st) around. (66)
Rnd 13-22: Sc in each st around.
Rnd 23: Sc in next 2 sts, sc next 2 sts tog, (sc in next 4
sts, sc next 2 sts tog) 10 times, sc in next 2 sts. (55)
Rnd 24: (Sc in next 3 sts, sc next 2 sts tog) around. (44)
Rnd 25: (Sc in next 9 sts, sc next 2 sts tog) around,
join with sl st in first st, leave long end for sewing,
fasten off. (40)
Insert eyes 8 sts apart between rnds 17-18.

Base

Rnd 1: With **fondant 052**, ch 2, 6 sc in second ch
from hook. (6)
Rnd 2: 2 sc in each st around. (12)
Rnd 3: (Sc in next st, 2 sc in next st) around. (18)
Rnd 4: (Sc in next 2 sts, 2 sc in next st) around. (24)
Rnd 5: (2 sc in next st, sc in next 3 sts) around. (30)
Rnd 6: Sc in next 2 sts, 2 sc in next st, (sc in next 4
sts, 2 sc in next st) 5 times, sc in next 2 sts. (36)
Rnd 7: Sc in next 4 sts, 2 sc in next st,
(sc in next 8 sts, 2 sc in next st) 3 times,
sc in next 4 sts, join with sl st in first st,
leave long end for sewing, fasten off. (40)

Sew Base to Body and stuff before sewing the opening
close.

Use pin to mark the middle between eyes. With **black** embroidery floss embroider mouth as in pictures.

Stuff the Tentacles and sew the opening close.

Sew the Tentacles around the Base.

Tentacle
Make 6.

Rnd 1: With **fondant 052**, ch 2, 6 sc in second ch from hook. (6)
Rnd 2: 2 sc in each st around. (12)
Rnd 3: (Sc in next st, 2 sc in next st) around. (18)
Rnd 4-6: Sc in each st around. (18)
Rnd 7: Sc in each st around, join with sl st in first st, leave long end for sewing, fasten off. (18)

Turtle

Size
Turtle's body has 7.5 inches (18.75 cm) diameter.

Note
Crochet using 2 strands of yarn and 5 mm hook.

Materials
- DK, Light Worsted
  Robin DK: Aqua 130 = 80 g and Fondant 052 = 15 g.
- 5.00 mm hook
- Polyester fiberfill = 80 g
- One pair of 12 mm safety eyes
- DMC Pearl Cotton Thread
  Size 3 (115/3): Color Black 310
- Tapestry needle

Body
Rnd 1: With **fondant 052**, ch 2, 6 sc in second ch from hook, changing to **aqua 130** in last 2 loops of last st. (6)
Rnd 2: 2 sc in each st around, changing to **fondant** in last 2 loops of last st. (12)
Rnd 3: (Sc in next st, 2 sc in next st) around, changing to **aqua** in last 2 loops of last st. (18)
Rnd 4: (Sc in next 2 sts, 2 sc in next st) around, changing to **fondant** in last 2 loops of last st. (24)

Rnd 5: (2 sc in next st, sc in next 3 sts) around, changing to **aqua** in last 2 loops of last st. (30)
Rnd 6: Sc in next 2 sts, 2 sc in next st, (sc in next 4 sts, 2 sc in next st) 5 times, sc in next 2 sts, changing to **fondant** in last 2 loops of last st. (36)
Rnd 7: (Sc in next 5 sts, 2 sc in next st) around, changing to **aqua** in last 2 loops of last st. (42)
Rnd 8: Sc in next 3 sts, 2 sc in next st, (sc in next 6 sts, 2 sc in next st) 5 times, sc in next 3 sts, changing to **fondant** in last 2 loops of last st. (48)
Rnd 9: (Sc in next 7 sts, 2 sc in next st) around, changing to **aqua** in last 2 loops of last st. (54)
Rnd 10: Sc in next 4 sts, 2 sc in next st, (sc in next 8 sts, 2 sc in next st) 5 times, sc in next 4 sts, changing to **fondant** in last 2 loops of last st. (60)
Rnd 11: (Sc in next 9 sts, 2 sc in next st) around, changing to **aqua** in last 2 loops of last st. (66)
Rnd 12: Sc in next 5 sts, 2 sc in next st, (sc in next 10 sts, 2 sc in next st) 5 times, sc in next 5 sts, changing to **fondant** in last 2 loops of last st. (72)
Rnd 13: (Sc in next 11 sts, 2 sc in next st) around, changing to **aqua** in last 2 loops of last st. (78)
Rnd 14: Sc in next 6 sts, 2 sc in next st, (sc in next 12 sts, 2 sc in next st) 5 times, sc in next 6 sts, changing to **fondant** in last 2 loops of last st. (84)
Rnd 15: Sc in each st around, changing to **aqua** in last 2 loops of last st.
Rnd 16-18: Sc in each st around.
Rnd 19: Sc in each st around, join with sl st in first st, fasten off.

Bottom
Rnd 1: With **aqua 130**, ch 2, 6 sc in second chain from hook. (6)
Rnd 2: 2 sc in each st around. (12)
Rnd 3: (Sc in next st, 2 sc in next st) around. (18)
Rnd 4: (Sc in next 2 sts, 2 sc in next st) around. (24)
Rnd 5: (2 sc in next st, sc in next 3 sts) around. (30)
Rnd 6: Sc in next 2 sts, 2 sc in next st, (sc in next 4 sts, 2 sc in next st) 5 times, sc in next 2 sts. (36)

Rnd 7: (Sc in next 5 sts, 2 sc in next st) around. (42)
Rnd 8: Sc in next 3 sts, 2 sc in next st, (sc in next 6 sts, 2 sc in next st) 5 times, sc in next 3 sts. (48)
Rnd 9: (Sc in next 7 sts, 2 sc in next st) around. (54)
Rnd 10: Sc in next 4 sts, 2 sc in next st, (sc in next 8 sts, 2 sc in next st) 5 times, sc in next 4 sts. (60)
Rnd 11: (Sc in next 9 sts, 2 sc in next st) around. (66)
Rnd 12: Sc in next 5 sts, 2 sc in next st, (sc in next 10 sts, 2 sc in next st) 5 times, sc in next 5 sts. (72)
Rnd 13: (Sc in next 11 sts, 2 sc in next st) around. (78)
Rnd 14: Sc in next 6 sts, 2 sc in next st, (sc in next 12 sts, 2 sc in next st) 5 times, sc in next 6 sts, join with sl st in first st, leave long end for sewing, fasten off. (84)

Sew Bottom to Body and stuff before sewing the opening close. Don't stuff to tight. I used 50 g of Polyester fiberfill for the Body.

Foot
Make 4 feets and do not stuff them.
Rnd 1: With **aqua 130**, ch 2, 4 sc in second ch from hook. (4)
Rnd 2: (2 sc in next st, sc in next st) 2 times. (6)
Rnd 3: Sc in next st, 2 sc in next 2 sts, sc in next 3 sts. (8)
Rnd 4: Sc in next 2 sts, 2 sc in next 2 sts, sc in next 4 sts. (10)
Rnd 5: Sc in next 3 sts, 2 sc in next 2 sts, sc in next 5 sts. (12)
Rnd 6: Sc in next 4 sts, 2 sc in next 2 sts, sc in next 6 sts. (14)
Rnd 7: Sc next 2 sts tog, sc in next 3 sts, 2 sc in next 2 sts, sc in next 3 sts, (sc next 2 sts tog) 2 times, leave long end for sewing, fasten off. (13)

Head
Rnd 1: With **aqua 130**, ch 2, 6 sc in second ch from hook. (6)
Rnd 2: 2 sc in each st around. (12)
Rnd 3: (Sc in next st, 2 sc in next st) around. (18)
Rnd 4: (Sc in next 2 sts, 2 sc in next st) around. (24)

Rnd 5: (2 sc in next st, sc in next 3 sts) around. (30)
Rnd 6: Sc in each st around.
Rnd 7: (Sc in next 4 sts, 2 sc in next st) around. (36)
Rnd 8-9: Sc in each st around. (36)
Rnd 10: (Sc in next 4 sts, sc next 2 sts tog) around.(30)
Rnd 11: (Sc in next 3 sts, sc next 2 sts tog) around. (24)
Rnd 12: (Sc in next 2 sts, sc next 2 sts tog) around. (18)
Rnd 13: (Sc in next st, sc next 2 sts tog) around. (12)

Insert eyes 6 sts apart between rnds 7-8. Stuff head tightly. With **black** embroidery floss embroider mouth as in picture.

Rnd 14-17: Sc in each st around. (12)
Rnd 18: Sc in next 4 sts, 2 sc in next st, sc in next 7 sts. (13)
Rnd 19-21: Sc in each st around. (13)
Rnd 22: Sc in each st around, leave long end for sewing, fasten off. (13)

Stuff neck loosely and sew the opening close.

Tail
Do not stuff tail.
Rnd 1: With **aqua 130**, ch 2, 4 sc in second ch from hook. (4)
Rnd 2: (2 sc in next st, sc in next st) 2 times. (6)
Rnd 3: Sc in each st around. (6)
Rnd 4: (Sc in next 2 sts, 2 sc in next st) 2 times, leave long end for sewing, fasten off. (8)

Finishing
Sew tail and head as in picture.

Sew back of head (rnd 14) to rnd 12 of the body.

Pin feet to the body and sew.

Fish

Materials

- DK, Light Worsted
  Robin DK: Fiesta 064 = 30 g
  Hayfield Baby Bonus DK: Pink 866 = 100 g
- 5.00 mm hook
- Polyester fiberfill = 200 g
- One pair of 15 mm safety eyes
- Tapestry needle

Size

Fish is 15 inches (37.5 cm) long.

Note

Crochet using 2 strands of yarn and 5 mm hook.

Body

Rnd 1: With **pink 866**, ch 2, 6 sc in second ch from hook. (6)
Rnd 2: 2 sc in each st around. (12)
Rnd 3: (Sc in next st, 2 sc in next st) around. (18)
Rnd 4: 2 sc in next 2 sts, sc in next 7 sts, 2 sc in next 2 sts, sc in next 7 sts. (22)
Rnd 5: Sc in next st, 2 sc in next 2 sts, sc in next 9 sts, 2 sc in next 2 sts, sc in next 8 sts. (26)
Rnd 6: Sc in next 2 sts, 2 sc in next 2 sts, sc in next 11 sts, 2 sc in next 2 sts, sc in next 9 sts. (30)
Rnd 7: Sc in next 3 sts, 2 sc in next 2 sts, sc in next 13 sts, 2 sc in next 2 sts, sc in next 10 sts. (34)
Rnd 8: Sc in next 4 sts, 2 sc in next 2 sts, sc in next 15 sts, 2 sc in next 2 sts, sc in next 11 sts. (38)
Rnd 9: Sc in next 5 sts, 2 sc in next 2 sts, sc in next 17 sts, 2 sc in next 2 sts, sc in next 12 sts. (42)

Rnd 10: Sc in next 6 sts, 2 sc in next 2 sts, sc in next 19sts, 2 sc in next 2 sts, sc in next 13 sts. (46)
Rnd 11: Sc in next 7 sts, 2 sc in next 2 sts, sc in next 21 sts, 2 sc in next 2 sts, sc in next 14 sts. (50)
Rnd 12-13: Sc in each st around.
Rnd 14: Sc in each st around, changing to **fiesta 064** in last 2 loops of last st.
Rnd 15: Sc in next 8 sts, 2 sc in next 2 sts, sc in next 23sts, 2 sc in next 2 sts, sc in next 15 sts. (54)
Rnd 16: Sc in each st around, changing to **pink 866** in last 2 loops of last st.
Rnd 17: Sc in next 9 sts, 2 sc in next 2 sts, sc in next 25 sts, 2 sc in next 2 sts, sc in next 16 sts. (58)
Rnd 18: Sc in each st around.
Rnd 19: Sc in next 10 sts, 2 sc in next 2 sts, sc in next 27 sts, 2 sc in next 2 sts, sc in next 17 sts. (62)
Rnd 20: Sc in each st around, changing to **fiesta 064** in last 2 loops of last st.
Rnd 21: Sc in next 11 sts, 2 sc in next 2 sts, sc in next 29 sts, 2 sc in next 2 sts, sc in next 18 sts. (66)
Rnd 22: Sc in each st around, changing to **pink 866** in last 2 loops of last st.
Rnd 23-25: Sc in each st around.
Rnd 26: Sc in each st around, changing to **fiesta 064** in last 2 loops of last st.
Rnd 27: Sc in each st around.
Rnd 28: Sc in each st around, changing to **pink 866** in last 2 loops of last st.
Rnd 29-31: Sc in each st around.
Rnd 32: Sc in each st around, changing to **fiesta 064** in last 2 loops of last st.
Rnd 33: Sc in each st around.

Rnd 34: Sc in each st around, changing to **pink 866** in last 2 loops of last st.

Rnd 35-37: Sc in each st around.

Rnd 38: Sc in each st around, changing to **fiesta 064** in last 2 loops of last st.

Rnd 39: Sc in next 16 sts, (sc next 2 sts tog) 2 times, sc in next 29 sts, (sc next 2 sts tog) 2 times, sc in next 13 sts. (62)

Rnd 40: Sc in each st around, changing to **pink 866** in last 2 loops of last st.

Rnd 41: Sc in next 15 sts, (sc next 2 sts tog) 2 times, sc in next 27 sts, (sc next 2 sts tog) 2 times, sc in next 12 sts. (58)

Insert eyes between rnds 10-11 on both side as in picture. Stuff.

Rnd 42: Sc in each st around.

Rnd 43: Sc in next 14 sts, (sc next 2 sts tog) 2 times, sc in next 25 sts, (sc next 2 sts tog) 2 times, sc in next 11 sts. (54)

Rnd 44: Sc in each st around, changing to **fiesta 064** in last 2 loops of last st.

Rnd 45: Sc in next 13 sts, (sc next 2 sts tog) 2 times, sc in next 23 sts, (sc next 2 sts tog) 2 times, sc in next 10 sts. (50)

Rnd 46: Sc in each st around, changing to **pink 866** in last 2 loops of last st.

Rnd 47: Sc in next 12 sts, (sc next 2 sts tog) 2 times, sc in next 21 sts, (sc next 2 sts tog) 2 times, sc in next 9 sts. (46)

Rnd 48: Sc in each st around.

Rnd 49: Sc in next 11 sts, (sc next 2 sts tog) 2 times, sc in next 19 sts, (sc next 2 sts tog) 2 times, sc in next 8 sts. (42)

Rnd 50: (Sc next 2 sts tog, sc in next 5 sts) around, changing to **fiesta 064** in last 2 loops of last st. (36)

Rnd 51: Sc in next 2 sts, sc next 2 sts tog, (sc in next 4 sts, sc next 2 sts tog) 5 times, sc in next 2 sts. (30)

Rnd 52: (Sc next 2 sts tog, sc in next 3 sts) around, changing to **pink 866** in last 2 loops of last st. (24)

Rnd 53: (Sc next 2 sts tog, sc in next 2 sts) around. Stuff. (18)

Rnd 54: (Sc next 2 sts tog, sc in next st) around. (12)

Rnd 55: Sc next 2 sts tog around. (6)

Rnd 56: Tail: 2 sc in each st around. (12)

Rnd 57: 2 sc in each st around. (24)

Rnd 58: (2 sc in next st, sc in next st) around. (36)

Rnd 59: Sc in each st around. (36)

Rnd 60: Tail part 1: Sc in next 7 sts, skip 18 sts, sc in next 11 sts. (18)

Rnd 61: Sc in each st around. (18)

Rnd 62: Sc in next 6 sts, sc next 2 sts tog, sc in next 7 sts, sc next 2 sts tog, sc in next st. (16)

Rnd 63: Sc in next 4 sts, sc next 2 sts tog, sc in next st, sc next 2 sts tog, sc in next 7 sts. (14)

Rnd 64: Sc in next 3 sts, sc next 2 sts tog, sc in next st, sc next 2 sts tog, sc in next 6 sts. (12)

Rnd 65: Sc in next 2 sts, sc next 2 sts tog, sc in next st, sc next 2 sts tog, sc in next 5 sts. (10)

Rnd 66: Sc in next st, sc next 2 sts tog, sc in next st, sc next 2 sts tog, sc in next 4 sts. (8)

Rnd 67: Sc next 2 sts tog, sc in next st, sc next 2 sts tog, sc in next 3 sts, sl st in first st, leave long end for sewing, fasten off. (6) Sew the opening close.

Tail part 2

Rnd 60: Join **pink 866** to next free st on rnd 59, ch 1, sc in same st, sc in next 17 sts. (18)

Rnd 61: Sc in each st around. (18)

Rnd 62: Sc in next 8 sts, sc next 2 sts tog, sc in next 6 sts, sc next 2 sts tog. (16)

Rnd 63: Sc in next st, sc next 2 sts tog, sc in next 11 sts, sc next 2 sts tog. (14)

Rnd 64: Sc in next st, sc next 2 sts tog, sc in next 9 sts, sc next 2 sts tog. (12)

Rnd 65: Sc in next st, sc next 2 sts tog, sc in next 7 sts, sc next 2 sts tog. (10)

42

Rnd 66: Sc in next st, sc next 2 sts tog, sc in next 5 sts, sc next 2 sts tog. (8)

Rnd 67: Sc in next st, sc next 2 sts tog, sc in next 3 sts, sc next 2 sts tog, sl st in first st, leave long end for sewing, fasten off. (6) Sew the opening close.

Flatten the mouth, fold in half and sew (see pictures).

Mouth

Rnd 1: With **pink 866**, ch 4, sc in second ch from hook, sc in next ch, 3 sc in next ch, working in remaining loops on opposite side of starting ch, sc in next ch, 2 sc in next ch. (8)

```
    x   x   x   o          o = ch
  x   o   o   o   x        x = sc
    x   x   x
```

Rnd 2: 2 sc in each st around. (16)
Rnd 3: Sc in each st around. (16)
Rnd 4: Sc next 2 sts tog around, sl st in first st, leave long end for sewing, fasten off. (8)

Sew mouth over rnds 1-2 of the body.

Sammy the Dog

Materials

- DK, Light Worsted
  Robin DK: Black 044 = 20 g,
  Jaffa 063 (orange) = 40 g and
  Spearmint 057 (light green) = 55 g
- 5.00 mm hook
- Polyester fiberfill = 170 g
- Black embroidery floss (or use one strand of
  black DK yarn)
- Tapestry needle
- Two 15 mm black buttons for eyes
- One 24 mm black button for nose
- Pins

Size

Sammy is 10 inches tall (25 cm).

Leg

Make 2.

Rnd 1: With **jaffa 063**, ch 2, 6 sc in second chain from hook. (6)
Rnd 2: (2 sc in next st, sc in next st) around. (9)
Rnd 3: (2 sc in next st, sc in next 2 sts) around. (12)
Rnd 4: (2 sc in next st, sc in next 3 sts) around. (15)
Rnd 5: (2 sc in next st, sc in next 4 sts) around, join with sl st in first st, fasten off. (18)

Body

Rnd 1: With **spearmint 057,** hold legs together. Insert hook in the center of first leg, pull out the loop from second leg, ch 1, sc in same st (do not count this stitch just for connecting legs together), sc in next 17 sts on second leg (mark first st), sc in next 17 sts on first leg. (34) See diagram for connecting legs together on page 6.

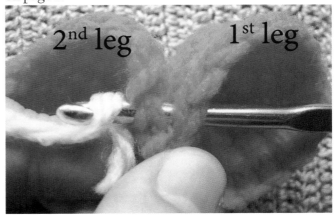

Rnd 2: (2 sc in next st, sc in next 16 sts) 2 times. (36)
Rnd 3: (Sc in next 5 sts, 2 sc in next st) around. (42)
Rnd 4: Sc in next 3 sts, 2 sc in next st, (sc in next 6 sts, 2 sc in next st) 5 times, sc in next 3 sts, changing to **jaffa 063** in last 2 loops of last st. (48)
Rnd 5-7: Sc in each st around.
Rnd 8: Sc in each st around, changing to **spearmint 057** in last 2 loops of last st.
Rnd 9-11: Sc in each st around.
Rnd 12: Sc in each st around, changing to **jaffa 063** in last 2 loops of last st.
Rnd 13-15: Sc in each st around
Rnd 16: (Sc next 2 sts tog, sc in next 6 sts) around, changing to **spearmint 057** in last 2 loops of last st. (42)
Rnd 17: Sc in each st around.

Rnd 18: (Sc in next 5 sts, sc next 2 sts tog) around. (36)
Rnd 19: Sc in each st around.
Rnd 20: Sc in next 2 sts, sc next 2 sts tog, (sc in next 4 sts, sc next 2 sts tog) 5 times, sc in next 2 sts, changing to jaffa 063 in last 2 loops of last st. (30)
Rnd 21-22: Sc in each st around.
Rnd 23: (Sc next 2 sts tog, sc in next 3 sts,) around, join with sl st in first st. Leave long end for sewing, fasten off. (24) Stuff body.

Head

Rnd 1: With spearmint 057, ch 2, 6 sc in second chain from hook. (6)
Rnd 2: 2 sc in each st around. (12)
Rnd 3: (2 sc in next st, sc in next st) around. (18)
Rnd 4: (2 sc in next st, sc in next 2 sts) around. (24)
Rnd 5: (2 sc in next st, sc in next 3 sts) around. (30)
Rnd 6: (2 sc in next st, sc in next 4 sts) around. (36)
Rnd 7: (2 sc in next st, sc in next 5 sts) around. (42)
Rnd 8-11: Sc in each st around.
Rnd 12: (2 sc in next st, sc in next 6 sts) around, changing to jaffa 063 in last 2 loops of last st. (48)
Rnd 13-15: Sc in each st around.
Rnd 16: Sc in each st around, changing to spearmint 057 in last 2 loops of last st. (48)
Rnd 17-19: Sc in each st around.
Rnd 20: Sc in each st around, changing to jaffa 063 in last 2 loops of last st. (48)
Rnd 21-23: Sc in each st around.
Rnd 24: Sc in each st around, changing to spearmint 057 in last 2 loops of last st. (48)
Rnd 25: Sc in each st around.
Rnd 26: (Sc in next 6 sts, sc next 2 sts tog) around. (42)
Rnd 27: Sc in each st around. Stuff.
Rnd 28: Sc in next 3 sts, sc next 2 sts tog, (sc in next 5 sts, sc next 2 sts tog) 5 times, sc in next 2 sts, changing to jaffa 063 in last 2 loops of last st. (36)
Rnd 29: (Sc next 2 sts tog, sc in next 4 sts) around. (30)
Rnd 30: (Sc in next 3 sts, sc next 2 sts tog) around. (24)

Rnd 31: (Sc in next 2 sts, sc next 2 sts tog) around. Stuff. (18)
Rnd 32: (Sc next 2 sts tog, sc in next st) around. (12)
Rnd 33: Sc next 2 sts tog around, join with sl st in first st, fasten off. Sew opening close. (6)
Pin head to body; the opening of body is covered by rnds 17-24 of head. Sew head to body.

Ear
Make 2.

Rnd 1: With black, ch 2, 6 sc in second chain from hook. (6)
Rnd 2: 2 sc in each st around. (12)
Rnd 3: (2 sc in next st, sc in next st) around. (18)
Rnd 4: (2 sc in next st, sc in next 2 sts) around. (24)
Rnd 5-7: Sc in each st around.
Rnd 8: (Sc in next 2 sts, sc next 2 sts tog) around. (18)
Rnd 9-11: Sc in each st around.
Rnd 12: (Sc next 2 sts tog, sc in next 4 sts) around. (15)
Rnd 13: Sc in each st around.
Rnd 14: (Sc in next 3 sts, sc next 2 sts tog) around. (12)
Rnd 15: Sc in each st around.
Rnd 16: Sc in each st around, join with sl st in first st. Leave long end for sewing, fasten off.
Sew the opening close flat. Pin ears 14 sts apart over rnds 19-24 of head. Sew ears to head.

Arm

Make 2, do not stuff arms.

Rnd 1: With **spearmint 057**, ch 2, 6 sc in second chain from hook. (6)

Rnd 2-11: Sc in each st around.

Rnd 12: Sc in each st around, join with sl st in first st. Leave long end for sewing, fasten off.

Sew arms to body on rnd 23 of body.

Finishing

Sew eyes (15 mm black buttons) 9 sts apart between rnds 16-17 of head.

Sew nose (24 mm black button) over rnds 2-5 of head.

Mouth

With **black** embroidery floss (or use one strand of **black** DK yarn), embroider mouth:

First: the needle comes out from under the nose button (number 1), goin to the head between rnds 7-8 (number 2) then come out between rnds 8-9 (number 3), goin to the head again at number 2 then come out between rnds 8-9 (number 4), goin to head again at number 2 then come out under the nose button, secure the embroidery floss, fasten off.

Froggy

Materials

- DK, Light Worsted
  Hayfield Baby Bonus DK: Baby Mint 853 = 70 g,
  Baby Pink 851 = 20 g, Baby Rose 867 = 70 g and
  Baby White 856 = 10 g.
- 5.00 mm hook (US: H/8, UK: 6)
- 15 mm safety eyes
- Polyester fiberfill = 275 g
- Tapestry needle
- Black embroidery floss

Size

Froggy is 18 inches/ 45 cm high (standing).

Note

Crochet using 2 strands of yarn. If you use Worsted
weight yarn, crochet using 1 strand of yarn.

Body

Rnd 1: With 2 strands of **baby rose 867,** ch 16, sc in
second ch from hook, sc in next 13 chs, 3 sc in next ch,
working in remaining loops on opposite side of
starting ch, sc in next 13 chs, 2 sc in next ch. (32)

```
      x   x   x   .   .   .   .   .   x   x   x   o
  x   o   o   o   .   .   .   .   .   o   o   o   x
      x   x   x   .   .   .   .   .   x   x   x
  x = sc                       o = ch
```

Rnd 2: (Sc in next st, 2 sc in next st) around. (48)
Rnd 3: Sc in each st around.
Rnd 4: (Sc in next 7 sts, 2 sc in next st) around. (54)
Rnd 5-8: Sc in each st around.
Rnd 9: <u>Working in back loops only.</u> (Sc in next 7 sts,
sc next 2 sts tog) around. (48)
Rnd 10: Sc in each st around.
Rnd 11: Sc in next 3 sts, sc next 2 sts tog, (sc in next
6 sts, sc next 2 sts tog) 5 times, sc in next 3 sts. (42)
Rnd 12: Sc in each st around.
Rnd 13: (Sc in next 5 sts, sc next 2 sts tog) around.(36)
Rnd 14-17: Sc in each st around.
Rnd 18: Sc in each st around, changing to
baby pink 851 in last 2 loops of last st.
Rnd 19: (Sc in next 4 sts , sc next 2 sts tog)
around.(30)

Rnd 20-22: Sc in each st around.
Rnd 23: (Sc in next 3 sts, sc next 2 sts tog)
around. (24)
Rnd 24: Sc in each st around. Stuff.
Rnd 25: (Sc in next 2 sts, sc next 2 sts tog)
around. (18)
Rnd 26-27: Sc in each st around.
Rnd 28: Sc in each st around, join with sl st in first st,
leave long end for sewing, fasten off. (18)

Skirt

Rnd 1: Join 2 strands of **baby rose 867** to free loop of rnd 8, ch 1, sc in same st, sc in next 7 sts, 2 sc in next st, (sc in next 8 sts, 2 sc in next st) 5 times. (60)

Rnd 2-3: Sc in each st around.
Rnd 4: (Sc in next 9 sts, 2 sc in next st) around. (66)
Rnd 5-10: Sc in each st around.
Rnd 11: Sl st in next st, (ch 2, 2 hdc in the same st, skip one st, sl st in next st) around. Fasten off.

Head

Rnd 1: With 2 strands of **baby mint 853**, ch 2, 6 sc in second chain from hook. (6)
Rnd 2: 2 sc in each st around. (12)
Rnd 3: (Sc in next st, 2 sc in next st) around. (18)
Rnd 4: (2 sc in next st, sc in next 2 sts) around. (24)
Rnd 5: (Sc in next 3 sts, 2 sc in next st) around. (30)
Rnd 6: Sc in next 2 sts, 2 sc in next st, (sc in next 4 sts, 2 sc in next st) 5 times, sc in next 2 around. (36)
Rnd 7: (Sc in next 5 sts, 2 sc in next st) around. (42)
Rnd 8: Sc in next 3 sts, 2 sc in next st, (sc in next 6 sts, 2 sc in next st) 5 times, sc in next 3 sts. (48)
Rnd 9: (Sc in next 7 sts, 2 sc in next st) around. (54)
Rnd 10: Sc in next 4 sts, 2 sc in next st, (sc in next 8 sts, 2 sc in next st) 5 times, sc in next 4 sts. (60)
Rnd 11-17: Sc in each st around.
Rnd 18: Sc in next 4 sts, sc next 2 sts tog, (sc in next 8 sts, sc next 2 sts tog) 5 times, sc in next 4 sts. (54)
Rnd 19: (Sc in next 7 sts, sc next 2 sts tog) around. (48)
Rnd 20: Sc in next 3 sts, sc next 2 sts tog, (sc in next 6 sts, sc next 2 sts tog) 5 times, sc in next 3 sts. (42)
Rnd 21: (Sc in next 5 sts, sc next 2 sts tog) around. (36)
Rnd 22: Sc in next 2 sts, sc next 2 sts tog, (sc in next 4 sts, sc next 2 sts tog) 5 times, sc in next 2 sts. (30)
Rnd 23: (Sc in next 3 sts, sc next 2 sts tog) around. Stuff. (24)
Rnd 24: (Sc in next 2 sts, sc next 2 sts tog) around, join with sl st in first st. Fasten off. (18)

Eye

Eyelid

Make 2.

Rnd 1: With 2 strands of **baby mint 853**, ch 2, 6 sc in second chain from hook. (6)
Rnd 2: 2 sc in each st around. (12)
Rnd 3: (Sc in next st, 2 sc in next st) around. (18)
Rnd 4: Sc in each st around.
Rnd 5: Sc in each st around, fasten off.

Eyeball

Make 2.

Rnd 1: With 2 strands of **baby white 856**, ch 2, 5 sc in second chain from hook. (5)
Rnd 2: 2 sc in each st around. (10)
Rnd 3: (Sc in next st , 2 sc in next st) around. (15)
Rnd 4: Sc in each st around.
Rnd 5: Sc in each st around, fasten off.

Insert safety eye in the middle of eyeball.

Stuff eyeball and put it inside the eyelid and sew them together.

Sew eyes on top of head over rnds 4-5 from middle top of head.

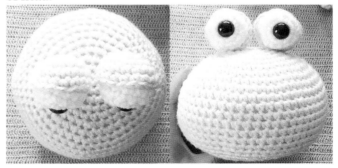

Use pins to mark a mouth line, mark 14 sts apart between rnds 10-11 from of head, one pin in the middle between rnds 14-15. With **black**, embroider mouth. Sew head to body.

Arm
Make 2.

Rnd 1: With 2 strands of **baby mint 853**, ch 2, 6 sc in second chain from hook. (6)
Rnd 2: (2 sc in next st, sc in next st) around. (9)
Rnd 3-5: Sc in each st around. Stuff.
Rnd 6: (Sc next 2 sts tog, sc in next st) around. (6)
Rnd 7-12: Sc in each st around. Stuff.
Rnd 13: Sc in each st around, changing to **baby pink 851** in last 2 loops of last st.
Rnd 14: (2 sc in next st, sc in next st) around. (9)
Rnd 15: Working in back loops only.
Sc in each st around.
Rnd 16-19: Sc in each st around. Stuff.
Rnd 20: (Sc in next st, sc next 2 sts tog) around, join with sl st in first st. Leaving long end for sewing, fasten off. Sew the opening close. (6)

Edge of sleeve
Join **baby pink 851** to free loop of rnd 14, (ch 3, sc in next st) around. Fasten off.
Sew rnds 19-20 of arms to rnds 26-27 of body.

Foot and Leg
Make 2, only stuff foot and do not stuff leg.

Rnd 1: With 2 strands of **baby rose 867**, ch 6, sc in second chain from hook, sc in next 3 chs, 3 sc in next ch, working in remaining loops on opposite side of starting ch, sc in next 3 chs, 2 sc in next ch. (12)

```
x x x x x o        o = ch
x o o o o o x      x = sc
  x x x x x
```

Rnd 2: 2 sc in next st, sc in next 3 sts, 2 sc in next 3 sts, sc in next 3 sts, 2 sc in next 2 sts. (18)
Rnd 3: Sc in next st, 2 sc in next st, sc in next 3 sts, (sc in next st, 2 sc in next st) 3 times, sc in next 3 sts, (sc in next st, 2 sc in next st) 2 times. (24)
Rnd 4-5: Sc in each st around.
Rnd 6: Sc in next 7 sts, sc next 2 sts tog, sc next 3 sts tog, sc next 2 sts tog, sc in next 10 sts, changing to **baby mint 853** in last 2 loops of last st. (20)
Rnd 7: Working in back loops only. Sc in next 3 sts, (sc next 2 sts tog) 5 times, sc in next 7 sts. (15)
Rnd 8: Sc in next 3 sts, sc next 2 sts tog, sc in next st, sc next 2 sts tog, sc in next 7 sts. Stuff. (13)
Rnd 9: Sc in next 3 sts, (sc next 2 sts tog) 3 times, sc in next 4 sts. (10)
Rnd 10: Sc in next 2 sts, (sc next 2 sts tog) 2 times, sc in next 4 sts. (8)
Rnd 11: Sc in next 2 sts, sc next 2 sts tog, sc in next 4 sts. (7)
Rnd 12-22: Sc in each st around.
Rnd 23: Sc in each st around, join with sl st in first st. Fasten off. Sew the opening close.

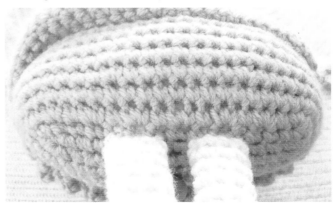

Sew legs to bottom of body.

Hunny & Funny Bunnies

Hunny Bunny

Body

Rnd 1: With **pink 046,** ch 27, sc in second ch from hook, sc in next 24 chs, 3 sc in next ch; working in remaining loops on opposite side of chain, sc in next 24 chs, 2 sc in next ch.(54)

```
X X X . . . . . X X X o
x o o o . . . . o o o x
  X X X . . . . . X X X
```

x = sc   o = ch

Rnd 2: 2 sc in next st, sc in next 24 sts, 2 sc in next 3 sts, sc in next 24 sts, 2 sc in next 2 sts. (60)

Rnd 3: Sc in next st, 2 sc in next st, sc in next 25 sts, 2 sc in next st, (sc in next st, 2 sc in next st) 2 times, sc in next 25 sts, 2 sc in next st, sc in next st, 2 sc in next st. (66)

Rnd 4: Sc in each st around.

Rnd 5: Sc in next 2 sts, 2 sc in next st, sc in next 26 sts, (2 sc in next st, sc in next 2 sts) 2 times, 2 sc in next st, sc in next 26 sts, 2 sc in next st, sc in next 2 sts, 2 sc in next st. (72)

Rnd 6: Sc in each st around.

Rnd 7: Sc in next 3 sts, 2 sc in next st, sc in next 27 sts, (2 sc in next st, sc in next 3 sts) 2 times, 2 sc in next st, sc in next 27 sts, 2 sc in next st, sc in next 3 sts, 2 sc in next st. (78)

Rnd 8-24: Sc in each st around.

Rnd 25: (Sc in next 11 sts, sc next 2 sts tog) around. (72)

Rnd 26: Sc in each st around.

Rnd 27: Sc in next 5 sts, sc next 2 sts tog, (sc in next 10 sts, sc next 2 sts tog) 5 times, sc in next 5 sts. (66)

Rnd 28: Sc in each st around.

Rnd 29: (Sc in next 9 sts, sc next 2 sts tog) around. (60)

Rnd 30: Sc in each st around.

Rnd 31: Sc in next 4 sts, sc next 2 sts tog, (sc in next 8 sts, sc next 2 sts tog) 5 times, sc in next 4 sts. (54)

Rnd 32: Sc in each st around.

Rnd 33: (Sc in next 7 sts, sc next 2 sts tog) around. (48)

Rnd 34: Sc in each st around.

Materials

- Chunky, Craft, Rug
  Robin FX Chunky: Tulip 4204 = 30 g
  Robin Chunky: Pink 046 = 130 g,
  Blue Madonna 033 = 35 g and Pale Blue 047 = 140 g
- 6.00 mm hook and 3 mm hook
- DMC Pearl Cotton Thread Size 3 (115/3):
  Color Pink 3326, Black 310 and Red 666
- Polyester fiberfill = 400 g (200 g/ doll)
- 2 pairs of 15 mm Black safety eyes
- Tapestry needle
- Pins

Size

Bunnies are 10 inches/ 25 cm high (excluding ears).

Note

Bunnies have same basic patterns for Body and Ears.

Rnd 35: Sc in next 3 sts, sc next 2 sts tog, (sc in next 6 sts, sc next 2 sts tog) 5 times, sc in next 3 sts. (42)
Rnd 36: Sc in each st around.
Rnd 37: (Sc in next 5 sts, sc next 2 sts tog) around.(36)
Rnd 38: Sc in each st around.

Put safety eyes 5 sts apart, between rnd 34-35 of body. Stuff.

Rnd 39: (Sc in next 4 sts, sc next 2 sts tog) around.(30)
Rnd 40: (Sc in next 3 sts, sc next 2 sts tog) around. Stuff. (24)
Rnd 41: (Sc in next 2 sts, sc next 2 sts tog) around. (18)
Rnd 42: (Sc in next st, sc next 2 sts tog) around. Stuff. (12)
Rnd 43: Sc next 2 sts tog around, join with sl st in first st, leave long end for sewing, fasten off. (6)
Sew the opening close.

Ear
Rnd 1: With **pink 046**, ch 2, 6 sc in second chain from hook. (6)
Rnd 2: (Sc in next st, 2 sc in next st) around, changing to **tulip 4204** in last 2 loops of last st. (9)
Rnd 3: (2 sc in next st, sc in next 2 sts) around. (12)
Rnd 4: (Sc in next 3 sts, 2 sc in next st) around, changing to **pink 046** in last 2 loops of last st. (15)

Rnd 5: Sc in next 2 sts, 2 sc in next st, (sc in next 4 sts, 2 sc in next st) 2 times, sc in next 2 sts. (18)
Rnd 6: (Sc in next 5 sts, 2 sc in next st) around, changing to **tulip 4204** in last 2 loops of last st. (21)
Rnd 7: Sc in next 3 sts, 2 sc in next st, (sc in next 6 sts, 2 sc in next st) 2 times, sc in next 3 sts. (24)
Rnd 8: (Sc in next 7 sts, 2 sc in next st) around, changing to **pink 046** in last 2 loops of last st. (27)
Rnd 9: Sc in each st around. (27)
Rnd 10: Sc in each st around, changing to **tulip 4204** in last 2 loops of last st. (27)
Rnd 11: Sc in each st around. (27)
Rnd 12: Sc in each st around, changing to **pink 046** in last 2 loops of last st. (27)
Rnd 13: Sc in each st around. (27)
Rnd 14: Sc in each st around, changing to **tulip 4204** in last 2 loops of last st. (27)
Rnd 15: Sc in each st around. (27)
Rnd 16: Sc in each st around, changing to **pink 046** in last 2 loops of last st. (27)
Rnd 17: Sc in each st around. (27)
Rnd 18: Sc in each st around, changing to **tulip 4204** in last 2 loops of last st. (27)
Rnd 19: Sc in each st around. (27)
Rnd 20: Sc in each st around, changing to **pink 046** in last 2 loops of last st. (27)
Rnd 21: (Sc next 2 sts tog, sc in next 7 sts) around. (24)
Rnd 22: Sc in each st around, changing to **tulip 4204** in last 2 loops of last st. (24)
Rnd 23: Sc in each st around. (24)
Rnd 24: Sc in next 3 sts, sc next 2 sts tog, (sc in next 6 sts, sc next 2 sts tog) 2 times, sc in next 3 sts, changing to **pink 046** in last 2 loops of last st. (21)
Rnd 25: Sc in each st around. (21)
Rnd 26: Sc in each st around, changing to **tulip 4204** in last 2 loops of last st. (21)
Rnd 27: (Sc next 2 sts tog, sc in next 5 sts) around. (18)
Rnd 28: Sc in each st around, changing to **pink 046** in last 2 loops of last st. (18)
Rnd 29: Sc in each st around. (18)
Rnd 30: Sc in next 2 sts, sc next 2 sts tog, (sc in next 4 sts, sc next 2 sts tog) 2 times, sc in next 2 sts, changing to **tulip 4204** in last 2 loops of last st. (15)
Rnd 31: Sc in each st around. (15)
Rnd 32: Sc in each st around, changing to **pink 046** in last 2 loops of last st. (15)
Rnd 33: (Sc next 2 sts tog, sc in next 3 sts) around. (12)
Rnd 34: Sc in each st around, changing to **tulip 4204** in last 2 loops of last st. (12)

Rnd 35: Sc in each st around. (12)
Rnd 36: (Sc next 2 sts tog, sc in next 2 sts) around, changing to **pink 046** in last 2 loops of last st. (9)
Rnd 37: Sc in each st around. (9)
Rnd 38: Sc in each st around, changing to **tulip 4204** in last 2 loops of last st. (9)
Rnd 39: (Sc next 2 sts tog, sc in next st) around. (6)
Rnd 40: Sc in each st around, changing to **pink 046** in last 2 loops of last st. (6)
Rnd 41-44: Sc in each st around. (6)
Rnd 45: Sc in each st around, changing to **tulip 4204** in last 2 loops of last st. (6)
Rnd 46: Sc in each st around. (6)
Rnd 47: (Sc in next st, 2 sc in next st) around, changing to **pink 046** in last 2 loops of last st. (9)
Rnd 48: Sc in each st around. (9)
Rnd 49: Sc in each st around, changing to **tulip 4204** in last 2 loops of last st. (9)
Rnd 50: (2 sc in next st, sc in next 2 sts) around. (12)
Rnd 51: Sc in each st around, changing to **pink 046** in last 2 loops of last st. (12)
Rnd 52: Sc in each st around. (12)
Rnd 53: (Sc in next 3 sts, 2 sc in next st) around, changing to **tulip 4204** in last 2 loops of last st. (15)
Rnd 54: Sc in each st around. (15)
Rnd 55: Sc in each st around, changing to **pink 046** in last 2 loops of last st. (15)
Rnd 56: Sc in next 2 sts, 2 sc in next st, (sc in next 4 sts, 2 sc in next st) 2 times, sc in next 2 sts. (18)
Rnd 57: Sc in each st around, changing to **tulip 4204** in last 2 loops of last st. (18)
Rnd 58: Sc in each st around. (18)
Rnd 59: (Sc in next 5 sts, 2 sc in next st) around, changing to **pink 046** in last 2 loops of last st. (21)
Rnd 60: Sc in each st around. (21)
Rnd 61: Sc in each st around, changing to **tulip 4204** in last 2 loops of last st.
Rnd 62: Sc in next 3 sts, 2 sc in next st, (sc in next 6 sts, 2 sc in next st) 2 times, sc in next 3 sts. (24)
Rnd 63: Sc in each st around, changing to **pink 046** in last 2 loops of last st. (24)
Rnd 64: Sc in each st around. (24)
Rnd 65: (Sc in next 7 sts, 2 sc in next st) around, changing to **tulip 4204** in last 2 loops of last st. (27)
Rnd 66: Sc in each st around. (27)
Rnd 67: Sc in each st around, changing to **pink 046** in last 2 loops of last st. (27)
Rnd 68: Sc in each st around. (27)
Rnd 69: Sc in each st around, changing to **tulip 4204** in last 2 loops of last st. (27)
Rnd 70: Sc in each st around. (27)
Rnd 71: Sc in each st around, changing to **pink 046** in last 2 loops of last st. (27)

Rnd 72: Sc in each st around. (27)
Rnd 73: Sc in each st around, changing to **tulip 4204** in last 2 loops of last st. (27)
Rnd 74: Sc in each st around. (27)
Rnd 75: Sc in each st around, changing to **pink 046** in last 2 loops of last st. (27)
Rnd 76: Sc in each st around. (27)
Rnd 77: Sc in each st around, changing to **tulip 4204** in last 2 loops of last st. (27)
Rnd 78: (Sc next 2 sts tog, sc in next 7 sts) around. (24)
Rnd 79: Sc in next 3 sts, sc next 2 sts tog, (sc in next 6 sts, sc next 2 sts tog) 2 times, sc in next 3 sts, changing to **pink 046** in last 2 loops of last st. (21)
Rnd 80: (Sc next 2 sts tog, sc in next 5 sts) around. (18)
Rnd 81: Sc in next 2 sts, sc next 2 sts tog, (sc in next 4 sts, sc next 2 sts tog) 2 times, sc in next 2 sts, changing to **tulip 4204** in last 2 loops of last st. (15)
Rnd 82: (Sc next 2 sts tog, sc in next 3 sts) around. (12)
Rnd 83: (Sc next 2 sts tog, sc in next 2 sts) around, changing to **pink 046** in last 2 loops of last st. (9)
Rnd 84: (Sc next 2 sts tog, sc in next st) around, join with sl st in first st, leave long end for sewing, fasten off. (6) Sew the opening close.

Heart

Make 2, working in rows.
Row 1: With DMC cotton perl no.3 thread **Deep Pink 3326** and 3.0mm hook, ch 2, 3 sc in second ch from hook, turn. (3)
Row 2: Ch 1, 2 sc in first st, sc in next st, 2 sc in next st, turn. (5)
Row 3: Ch 1, sc in each st across, turn. (5)
Row 4: Ch 1, 2 sc in first st, sc in next 3 sts, 2 sc in next st, turn. (7)
Row 5: Skip first st, 5 dc in next st, skip next st, sl st in next st, skip next st, 5 dc in next st, skip next st, sl st in next st, leave long end for sewing, fasten off.

Bow

Bow piece

Row 1: With **tulip 4204**, ch 2, 3 sc in second ch from hook, turn. (3)

Row 2: Ch 1, sc in each st across, turn. (3)

Row 3: Ch 1, 2 sc in first st, sc in next st, 2 sc in next st, turn. (5)

Row 4: Ch 1, 2 sc in first st, sc in next 3 sts, 2 sc in next st, turn. (7)

Row 5-12: Ch 1, sc in each st across, turn. (7)

Row 13: Ch 1, sc first 2 sts tog, sc in next 3 sts, sc next 2 sts tog, turn. (5)

Row 14: Ch 1, sc first 2 sts tog, sc in next st, sc next 2 sts tog, turn. (3)

Row 15-18: Ch 1, sc in each st across, turn. (3)

Row 19: Ch 1, 2 sc in first st, sc in next st, 2 sc in next st, turn. (5)

Row 20: Ch 1, 2 sc in first st, sc in next 3 sts, 2 sc in next st, turn. (7)

Row 21-28: Ch 1, sc in each st across, turn.(7)

Row 29: Ch 1, sc first 2 sts tog, sc in next 3 sts, sc next 2 sts tog, turn. (5)

Row 30: Ch 1, sc first 2 sts tog, sc in next st, sc next 2 sts tog, turn. (3)

Row 31: Ch 1, sc in each st across.

Row 32: Ch 1, sc 3 sts tog, leaving long end for sewing, fasten off. (1) Sew row 1 and row 32 of bow together.

Middle piece

Row 1: With **tulip 4204**, ch 6, sc in second chain from hook, sc in next 4 chs, turn. (5)

Row 2: Ch 1, sc in each st across.

Row 3: Ch 1, sc in each st across, leave long end for sewing, fasten off. Sew the middle piece around middle of bow.

Finishing

Sew middle of ears on middle top of Body.

Sew Bow on middle top as in picture.

With DMC cotton perl no.3 thread **red 666**, embroider mouth.

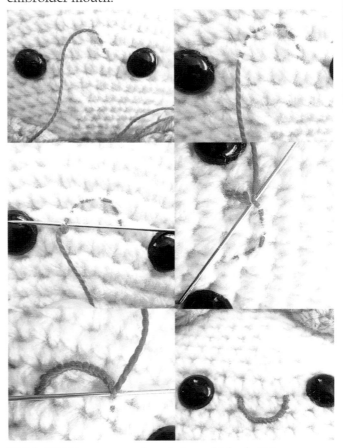

With DMC cotton perl no.3 thread **black 310**, embroider eyelashes.

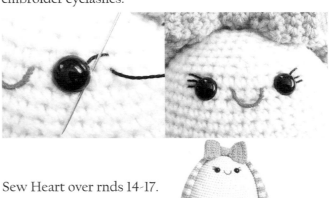

Sew Heart over rnds 14-17.

Funny Bunny

Body
Same as Hunny Bunny pattern.
Rnd 1- 43: pale blue 047.

Ear
Same as Hunny Bunny pattern.
Replace **pink 046** color with **pale blue 047**.
Replace **tulip 4204** color with **blue madonna 033**.

Mustache
With DMC cotton perl no.3 thread **black 310** and 3.0mm hook, ch16, sl st in second chain from hook, sc in next ch, hdc in next ch, dc in next ch, hdc in next ch, sc in next ch, sl st in next 3 chs, sc in next ch, hdc in next ch, dc in next ch, hdc in next ch, sc in next ch, sl st in next ch, leave long end for sewing, fasten off.

Finishing
Sew middle of ears on middle top of Body.
Sew Heart over rnds 14-17.

Pin Mustache between eyes and sew.

Hair
Cut 18 pieces of **pale blue 047** yarn, 6 inches long in length. Insert hair in 3 lines as marked in picture below.

Each line has 6 stands of yarn lined up.

Split yarn to make fluffy thin hair.

Baby Bunny

Materials

- DK, Light Worsted
  Bonny Baby DK from Robin: Pink 1361 = 65g
  Robin Paintbox DK: Tropics 1113 = 15 g
- 5.00 mm hook (US: H/8, UK: 6)
- Black embroidery floss
- Tapestry needle
- Pins
- Polyester fibrefill = 100g

Size
Baby Bunny is 10.4 inches (26 cm) tall
excluding ears.

Note
Crochet using 2 strands of yarn. If you use Worsted
weight yarn, crochet using 1 strand of yarn.

Head and Body
Work from top of the head to bottom of the body.
Crochet using 2 strands of yarn.
Rnd 1: With **pink 1361** (head color), ch 2,
6 sc in second chain from hook. (6)
Rnd 2: 2 sc in each st around. (12)
Rnd 3: (Sc in next st, 2 sc in next st) around. (18)
Rnd 4: (2 sc in next st, sc in next 2 sts) around. (24)
Rnd 5: (Sc in next 3 sts, 2 sc in next st) around. (30)
Rnd 6: Sc in next 2 sts, 2 sc in next st, (sc in next 4 sts,
2 sc in next st) 5 times, sc in next 2 sts. (36)
Rnd 7: (Sc in next 5 sts, 2 sc in next st) around. (42)
Rnd 8: Sc in each st around.
Rnd 9: Sc in next 3 sts, 2 sc in next st, (sc in next 6 sts,
2 sc in next st) 5 times, sc in next 3 sts. (48)
Rnd 10-15: Sc in each st around.
Rnd 16: (Sc in next 6 sts, sc next 2 sts tog)
around. (42)
Rnd 17: Sc in each st around.
Rnd 18: (Sc in next 5 sts, sc next 2 sts tog)
around. (36)
Rnd 19: (Sc in next 4 sts, sc next 2 sts tog)
around. (30)
Rnd 20: (Sc in next 3 sts, sc next 2 sts tog)
around. (24)
Rnd 21: (Sc in next 2 sts, sc next 2 sts tog)
around. (18)

Rnd 22: (Sc next 2 sts tog, sc in next st) around,
changing to **tropics 1113** (shirt color) in last 2 loops of
last st. (12)
Rnd 23: (Sc in next st, 2 sc in next st) around.
Stuff head. (18)
Rnd 24: (Sc in next 2 sts, 2 sc in next st) around. (24)
Rnd 25-32: Sc in each st around.
Rnd 33: Sc in each st around, changing to **pink 1361**
(body color) in last 2 loops of last st.
Rnd 34-35: Sc in each st around.
Rnd 36: (Sc in next 2 sts, sc next 2 sts tog) around.
Stuff body. (18)
Rnd 37: (Sc in next st, sc next 2 sts tog) around. (12)
Rnd 38: Sc next 2 sts tog around, join with sl st in first
st, fasten off. (6)

Arm
Make 2, crochet using 2 strands of yarn and
only stuff hand.
Rnd 1: With **pink 1361**, ch 2, 6 sc in second chain from
hook. (6)

Rnd 2: (Sc in next st, 2 sc in next st) around. (9)
Rnd 3: Sc in each st around.
Rnd 4: (Sc in next st, sc next 2 sts tog) around. Stuff. (6)
Rnd 5-8: Sc in each st around.
Rnd 9: Sc in each st around, join with sl st in first st. Leave long end for sewing, fasten off.
Sew arms to body on rnd 24.

Leg
Make 2, crochet using 2 strands of yarn and only stuff feet.

Rnd 1: With **pink 1361**, ch 2, 6 sc in second ch from hook. (6)
Rnd 2: 2 sc in each st around. (12)
Rnd 3: (Sc in next st, 2 sc in next st) around. (18)
Rnd 4: Sc in each st around.
Rnd 5: Sc in next 6 sts, (sc next 2 sts tog) 3 times, sc in next 6 sts. (15)
Rnd 6: Sc in next 3 sts, (sc next 2 sts tog) 2 times, sc in next st, (sc next 2 sts tog) 2 times, sc in next 3 sts. (11)
Rnd 7: Sc in next 4 sts, sc next 3 sts tog, sc in next 4 sts. Stuff. (9)
Rnd 8-11: Sc in each st around.
Rnd 12: Sc in each st around, join with sl st in first st. Leave long end for sewing, fasten off.

Sew legs to rnds 36-38 of body.

Ear
Make 2, crochet using 2 strands of yarn.

Rnd 1: With **pink 1361**, ch 2, 6 sc in second ch from hook. (6)
Rnd 2: 2 sc in each st around. (12)
Rnd 3: (Sc in next st, 2 sc in next st) around. (18)
Rnd 4: (2 sc in next st, sc in next 2 sts) around. (24)
Rnd 5-7: Sc in each st around.
Rnd 8: (Sc next 2 sts tog, sc in next 2 sts) around. (18)
Rnd 9: Sc in each st around.

Rnd 10: (Sc next 2 sts tog, sc in next st) around. (12)
Rnd 11: Sc in each st around.
Rnd 12: Sc next 2 sts tog around. (6)
Rnd 13: Sc in each st around, join with sl st in first st. Leave long end for sewing, fasten off. (6)

Bow
Crochet using 2 strands of yarn.

Rnd 1: With **tropics 1113**, ch 10, sc in second chain from hook, sc in next 3 chs, sl st in next ch, sc in next 3 chs, 4 sc in last ch; working in remaining loops on opposite side of chain, sc in next 3 chs, sl st in next ch, sc in next 3 chs, 3 sc in next ch, join with sl st in first st. (22)
Rnd 2: Ch 1, 2 sc in first st, sc in next 2 sts, sl st in next 3 sts, sc in next 2 sts, 2 sc in next 4 sts, sc in next 2 sts, sl st in next 3 sts, sc in next 2 sts, 2 sc in next 3 sts, join with sl st in first st. Leave long end for sewing, fasten off. (30)

Middle piece
Row 1: With **tropics 1113**, ch 4, sc in second ch from hook, turn. (3)
Row 2-3: Ch 1, sc in each st across, turn.
Row 4: Ch 1, sc in each st across, leave long end for sewing, fasten off.

Sew the middle piece around middle of bow.

Finishing
Sew ears on rnds 1-2 of head.

Sew bow in the middle between ears; sew bow to ears first then sew to head, see pictures.

With **black** embroidery floss, embroider eyes on rnd 10 and embroider nose on rnd 12 as in pictures.

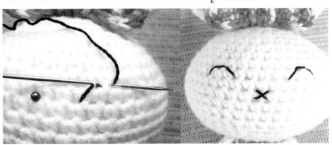

Baby Bear

Materials

- DK, Light Worsted
  Bonny Baby DK from Robin: Blue 1362 = 55 g,
  Pink 1361 = 5 g and Cream 1365 = 5 g
- 5.00 mm hook (US: H/8, UK: 6)
- Black embroidery floss
- Tapestry needle
- Pins
- Polyester fibrefill = 100g

Size

Baby Bear is 10.4 inches (26 cm) tall.

Head and Body

Work from top of the head to bottom of the body.
Crochet using 2 strands of yarn.

Rnd 1: With **blue 1362**, ch 2, 6 sc in second chain from hook. (6)
Rnd 2: 2 sc in each st around. (12)
Rnd 3: (Sc in next st, 2 sc in next st) around. (18)
Rnd 4: (2 sc in next st, sc in next 2 sts) around. (24)
Rnd 5: (Sc in next 3 sts, 2 sc in next st) around. (30)
Rnd 6: Sc in next 2 sts, 2 sc in next st, (sc in next 4 sts, 2 sc in next st) 5 times, sc in next 2 sts. (36)
Rnd 7: (Sc in next 5 sts, 2 sc in next st) around. (42)
Rnd 8: Sc in each st around.
Rnd 9: Sc in next 3 sts, 2 sc in next st, (sc in next 6 sts, 2 sc in next st) 5 times, sc in next 3 sts. (48)
Rnd 10-15: Sc in each st around.
Rnd 16: (Sc in next 6 sts, sc next 2 sts tog) around. (42)
Rnd 17: Sc in each st around.
Rnd 18: (Sc in next 5 sts, sc next 2 sts tog) around. (36)

Rnd 19: (Sc in next 4 sts, sc next 2 sts tog) around. (30)
Rnd 20: (Sc in next 3 sts, sc next 2 sts tog) around. (24)
Rnd 21: (Sc in next 2 sts, sc next 2 sts tog) around. (18)
Rnd 22: (Sc next 2 sts tog, sc in next st) around, changing to **pink 1361** in last 2 loops of last st. (12)
Rnd 23: (Sc in next st, 2 sc in next st) around, changing to **cream 1365** in last 2 loops of last st. Stuff head. (18)
Rnd 24: (Sc in next 2 sts, 2 sc in next st) around, changing to **blue 1362** in last 2 loops of last st. (24)
Rnd 25: Sc in each st around, changing to **pink 1361** in last 2 loops of last st.

Rnd 26: Sc in each st around, changing to **cream 1365** in last 2 loops of last st.
Rnd 27: Sc in each st around, changing to **blue 1362** in last 2 loops of last st.
Rnd 28: Sc in each st around, changing to **pink 1361** in last 2 loops of last st.
Rnd 29: Sc in each st around, changing to **cream 1365** in last 2 loops of last st.
Rnd 30: Sc in each st around, changing to **blue 1362** in last 2 loops of last st.
Rnd 31: Sc in each st around, changing to **pink 1361** in last 2 loops of last st.
Rnd 32: Sc in each st around, changing to **cream 1365** in last 2 loops of last st.
Rnd 33: Sc in each st around, changing to **blue 1362** in last 2 loops of last st.
Rnd 34-35: Sc in each st around.
Rnd 36: (Sc in next 2 sts, sc next 2 sts tog) around. Stuff body. (18)
Rnd 37: (Sc in next st, sc next 2 sts tog) around. (12)
Rnd 38: Sc next 2 sts tog around, join with sl st in first st, fasten off. (6)

Arm
Make 2, crochet using 2 strands of yarn and only stuff hand.
Rnd 1: With **blue 1362**, ch 2, 6 sc in second chain from hook. (6)
Rnd 2: (Sc in next st, 2 sc in next st) around. (9)
Rnd 3: Sc in each st around.
Rnd 4: (Sc in next st, sc next 2 sts tog) around. Stuff. (6)
Rnd 5-8: Sc in each st around.
Rnd 9: Sc in each st around, join with sl st in first st. Leave long end for sewing, fasten off.

Sew arms to body on rnd 24.

Leg
Make 2, crochet using 2 strands of yarn and only stuff feet.
Rnd 1: With **blue 1362**. Ch 2, 6 sc in second ch from hook. (6)
Rnd 2: 2 sc in each st around. (12)
Rnd 3: (Sc in next st, 2 sc in next st) around. (18)
Rnd 4: Sc in each st around.

Rnd 5: Sc in next 6 sts, (sc next 2 sts tog) 3 times, sc in next 6 sts. (15)
Rnd 6: Sc in next 3 sts, (sc next 2 sts tog) 2 times, sc in next st, (sc next 2 sts tog) 2 times, sc in next 3 sts. (11)
Rnd 7: Sc in next 4 sts, sc next 3 sts tog, sc in next 4 sts. Stuff. (9)
Rnd 8-11: Sc in each st around.
Rnd 12: Sc in each st around, join with sl st in first st. Leave long end for sewing, fasten off.

Sew legs to rnds 36-38 of body.

Ear
Make 2, crochet using 2 strands of yarn.
Rnd 1: With **blue 1362**, ch 2, 6 sc in second chain from hook. (6)
Rnd 2: 2 sc in each st around. (12)
Rnd 3: (Sc in next st, 2 sc in next st) around. (18)
Rnd 4: Sc in each st around.
Rnd 5: (Sc next 2 sts tog, sc in next st) around, join with sl st in first st. Leave long end for sewing, fasten off. (12) Sew the opening close.

Bear Muzzle
Crochet using 2 strands of yarn.
Rnd 1: With **cream 1365**, ch 2, 6 sc in second ch from hook. (6)
Rnd 2: 2 sc in each st around, join with sl st in first st. Leave long end for sewing, fasten off. (12)
With **black** embroidery floss, embroider nose and mouth (see page 6).

Finishing
Sew ears on rnds 8-13 of head.
Sew muzzle on rnds 12-16 of head.

How to embroider eyes is on the next page.

With **black** embroidery floss, embroider eyes on rnd 12 as in pictures.

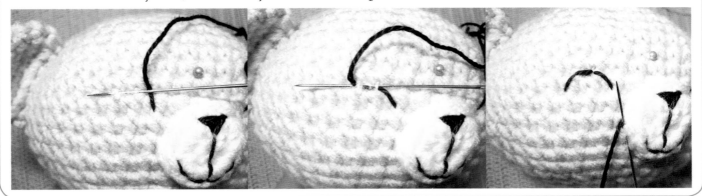

Easy Baby Blanket

Materials

- DK, Light Worsted
  Bonny Baby DK from Robin: Blue 1362 = 340 g,
  Pink 1361 = 40 g and Cream 1365 = 35 g
- 6.00 mm hook (US: J/10, UK: 4)
- Black embroidery floss
- Tapestry needle
- Pins
- Polyester fibrefill = 100g

Size

The blanket is 28x30 inches (71 x 76 cm)
Gauge: 16 sts and 16 rows = 4 inches (10 cm).

Note

- This project is working in rows, start with chain one and turn at the end of rows.
- Each sc and ch 1 is counted as 1 stitch.
- Crochet using 2 strands of yarn.

Blanket

Crochet using 2 strands of yarn.
Row 1: With **blue 1362**, ch 120, sc in second chain from hook, (ch 1, skip 1 ch, sc in next ch) repeat to end, turn. (119)
Row 2: Ch 1, sc in first sc, (sc in next ch space, ch 1, skip next sc) repeat to last 2 sts, sc in last ch space, sc in last sc, turn.
Row 3: Ch 1, sc in first sc, (ch 1, skip next sc, sc in next ch space) repeat to last 2 sts, ch 1, skip next sc, sc in last sc, turn.

Repeat rows 2 - 3 throughout working in the following color sequence:
Row 4-5: Use blue.
Row 6-7: Use pink.
Row 8-17: Use blue.
Row 18-19: Use cream.
Row 20-29: Use blue.
Row 30-31: Use pink.
Row 32-41: Use blue.
Row 42-43: Use cream.
Row 44-53: Use blue.
Row 54-55: Use pink.
Row 56-65: Use blue.
Row 66-67: Use cream.
Row 68-77: Use blue.
Row 78-79: Use pink.
Row 80-89: Use blue.
Row 90-91: Use cream.
Row 92-101: Use blue.
Row 102-103: Use pink.
Row 104-108: Use blue, fasten off after finish row 108.

Big doll
How to embroider mouth.

Small doll
How to embroider mouth.

How to join Yarn.
Join yarn to free loop, ch 1, sc in same st.

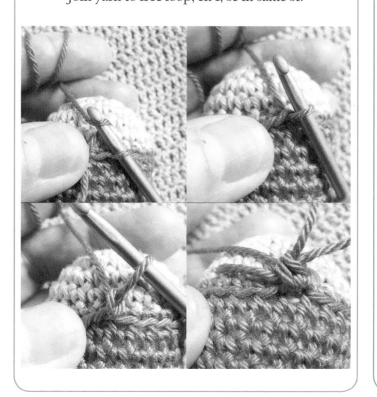

How to read pattern.

Rnd 4: (Sc in next 2 sts, 2 sc in next st) around. (24)
Number (24) at the end of round = number of stitches after finished round.

Rnd 5: (Sc in next 3 sts, 2 sc in next st) **around. (30)**
Repeat (Sc in next 3 sts, 2 sc in next st) until end of round
⇒ **Rnd 5:** (Sc in next 3 sts, 2 sc in next st), (Sc in next 3 sts, 2 sc in next st), (Sc in next 3 sts, 2 sc in next st), (Sc in next 3 sts, 2 sc in next st), (Sc in next 3 sts, 2 sc in next st), (Sc in next 3 sts, 2 sc in next st)
Total stitches of Rnd 5 = 5+5+5+5+5+5 = 30 sts

Rnd 6: Sc in next 2 sts, 2 sc in next st, (sc in next 4 sts, 2 sc in next st) 5 times, **sc in next 2 sts. (36)**
Repeat (sc in next 4 sts, 2 sc in next st) 5 times
⇒ **Rnd 6:** Sc in next 2 sts, 2 sc in next st, (sc in next 4 sts, 2 sc in next st), (sc in next 4 sts, 2 sc in next st), (sc in next 4 sts, 2 sc in next st), (sc in next 4 sts, 2 sc in next st), (sc in next 4 sts, 2 sc in next st), sc in next 2 sts.
Total stitches of Rnd 6 = 2+2+6+6+6+6+2 = 36 sts

The big bunny is a Huggy Bunny from the "Huggy Dolls Amigurumi".

Comparison color chart for Catania & DMC Petra No3		
Color	Catania	DMC Petra No3
cream	130	ECRU
red	115	5321
black	110	5310
white	106	B5200
light pink	246	54461
pink	222	54458
apple green	205	5907
jade	253	53814
green	241	5905
light brown	248	5712
purple	240	53837
light blue	173	54518
blue	247	5798
dark blue	164	5823
light yellow	100	53823
yellow	208	5745
orange	189	5608
dark brown	162	5938
light green	385	5772
taupe	254	5646

Huggy Dolls Amigurumi
Subtitle: 15 Huggable Doll Patterns
Publisher: K and J Publishing
Author: Sayjai Thawornsupacharoen
Publication date: 14th of June 2014
ISBN: 978-1910407028

Easy Amigurumi
Subtitle: 28 doll patterns
Publisher: K and J Publishing
Author: Sayjai Thawornsupacharoen
Publication date: 18th of July 2014
ISBN: 978-1910407011

Dress Up Dolls Amigurumi
Subtitle: 5 big dolls with clothes, shoes, accessories, tiny bear and big carry bag patterns
Publisher: K and J Publishing
Author: Sayjai Thawornsupacharoen
Publication date: 27th of September 2014
ISBN: 978-1910407066

Sunny Amigurumi
Subtitle: Crochet Patterns
Publisher: K and J Publishing
Author: Sayjai Thawornsupacharoen
Editor: Robert Appelboom
Date of publication: 25th of February 2015
ISBN: 978-1910407189

Yarn Weight System

	USA	UK	Australia	Recommended Hook in Metric (mm)
0 lace	Lace weight	1 ply	2 ply	1.5 - 2.25 mm
1 superfine	Fingering	2 ply	3 ply	2.25 - 3 mm
1 superfine	Sock	3 ply	3 ply	2.25 - 3.5 mm
2 fine	Sport	4 ply	5 ply	3.5 - 4.5 mm
3 light	DK, Light worsted	DK	8 ply	4.5 - 5.5 mm
4 medium	Worsted	Aran	10 ply	5.5 - 6.5 mm
5 bulky	Bulky	Chunky	12 ply	6.5 - 9 mm
6 super bulky	Super Bulky	Super Chunky	14 ply	9 mm and larger

Crochet Hook Size Conversion

Hook in Metric (mm)	USA	UK	Japanese
1.00 mm	10 steel	4 steel	4 steel
1.25 mm	8 steel	3 steel	2 steel
1.50 mm	7 steel	2.5 steel	--
1.75 mm	4 steel	2 steel	--
2.00 mm	--	14	2/0
2.25 mm	B/1	13	3/0
2.50 mm	--	12	4/0
2.75 mm	C/2	--	--
3.00 mm	--	11	5/0
3.25 mm	D/3	10	--
3.50 mm	E/4	9	6/0
3.75 mm	F/5	--	--
4.00 mm	G/6	8	7/0
4.50 mm	7	7	7.5/0
5.00 mm	H/8	6	8/0
5.50 mm	I/9	5	--
6.00 mm	J/10	4	10/0
6.50 mm	K/10.5	3	7
7.00 mm	--	2	--
8.00 mm	L/11	0	8
9.00 mm	M/13	00	9
10.00 mm	N/15	000	10

Copyright

First Edition
Date of publication: 27th of June 2015
Editor: Robert Appelboom
Publisher: K and J Publishing
Cambridge, England

http://kandjdolls.blogspot.co.uk

www.facebook.com/kandjdolls.amigurumi.patterns